DRUG ABUSE

DRUG ABUSE

Socio-Psychological Perspectives and Intervention Strategies

Dr. Rashmi Agrawal

SHIPRA

ISBN 81-85402-64-7

First Published in India in 1995

Published by :
SHIPRA PUBLICATIONS
115-A, Vikas Marg, Shakarpur
Delhi-110092 (India)
Phone : 2200954; 2458662

Laser Typeset at :
PRE PRINT SERVICES
Delhi-110026

Printed at :
Chaudhary Offset Process
Delhi-110051

This book is dedicated to my father late Sh. B.N. Agrawal and my mother Smt. Shanti Agrawal. I am indebted to them for having developed in me the consciousness that every individual owes something to the society which he or she must repay in a suitable manner. The book is also dedicated to the young boys and girls who heeded my counsel and helped themselves to come back in the mainstream of life and make valuable contributions in years to come.

Contents

Acknowledgements

I wish to express my deep sense of gratitude to the young men and women who had the misfortune of having been caught in the drugs net and confided in me about their drug-related behaviours. They include persons in India as well as in other countries. Discussions and counselling about their psychological compulsions and emotional problems enabled some of them to come out of the abuse. Their success stories have inspired me to write this book.

Special words of thanks are due to people who shared their own experiences about drug-trafficking and abuse. They include police personnel, doctors, social workers and senior officials involved in drug control and prevention programmes. All of them together helped me to gain an insight into the painful journey from addiction to recovery.

The United States Information Library and UNDCP provided material to enable me to have a contrastive analysis of the problems as they exist in India and other highly developed societies. I am thankful to them. Officers of the Ministry of Welfare, Government of India, deserve thanks for having provided relevant information regarding the extent of the abuse problem in India and the efforts being made at official level to contain it.

I acknowledge the enthusiastic support extended to me by my publishers who consented to publish the book knowing that it would be my first professional effort.

My heart-felt thanks are due to the members of my family and friends who extended loving care and concern while I was involved in this venture. Let all of them remain unnamed.

Lastly my affectionate concerns are due to my nephew 'Mausam' whose innocent querries motivated me to write a book that may also be useful to the non-professional reader.

Author's Note

The drugs problem is no longer confined to any specific geographical area or social class. Drug-related crimes and drug abuse continue unabated notwithstanding stricter laws, seizures, penalties and a number of solutions being put forth by various agencies acting at national and international levels. The drug menace has spread its tentacles to communities, workplaces, colleges and lastly schools. It appears nothing is going to work as a text-book solution. The problem has many dimensions and each dimension needs detailed study before humanity can dream of a world free from drugs as it marches into the twenty-first century.

Before strategies could be drawn to beat the drug sub-culture one has to have detailed information about the drug trafficking routes whose network is much more organised than the best operated railways or the international airways anywhere in the world. We, in India, have to identify the areas which are most prone to being used as conduits.

The percentage of people involved in India may be low but the fact remains that it is increasing rapidly. Public awareness about various drugs must increase simultaneously so that each one can play his or her role in identifying the new converts and ensuring that he or she is kept out and warned of the dangers well before addiction has set in.

For those whose near and dear ones are already in the net, it is important to know what the treatment strategies are and where one can get help.

Governments have to be aware of the difficulties involved in the way of drug control. Only then is the enforcement of laws possible.

The war on drugs has to be fought at the State level and also at the family level. Women, children and other more vulnerable sections of the society need special protection. This protection has to come from the community. At the community level, there is need for programmes that would disseminate knowledge about drug abuse prevention and techniques that would help the individuals to get out of the drug net if unfortunately they have got trapped into it. The individual must know how and why some people get into drugs while the rest manage to face problems courageously even though faced under similar adverse circumstances.

There are millions in the net. There are also thousands who have been able to come out. The success stories should be a source of strength to those who had the misfortune of having been addicted.

While the book was being written, I interviewed a cross-section of people in India and abroad. They talked in confidence and, as such, while their views have been faithfully recorded, their identity has been left disguised.

I have deliberately tried to avoid making extensive references from available literature on the subject except where it is very relevant. The statistics used have been obtained from a number of sources. Prominent among them are the documents issued by the United Nations Drug Control and Prevention Programme and the U.N. Drug Control Board. Statistics relating to India have been obtained, courtesy Narcotics Control Bureau and a number of newspapers and magazines.

I have tried to cover the multi-faceted gamut of drug-related problems, with special emphasis on the psychological aspects, and through them tried to comment upon strategies that are most likely to succeed in humanity's war against the menace.

The book is not a document of despair. It shows ways for effective prevention and treatment techniques. There are practical suggestions for parents, school teachers, community leaders and young men and women. These suggestions are based on success stories collected from different parts of the world including India and should go a long way in transforming lives of men and women in despair. Wherever that happens, the purpose of writing this book would have been amply served. Sometimes laws do not help, individuals can create wonders.

Introduction

Drug trafficking and abuse have now assumed global dimensions. India is no exception. The worst thing about drug abuse in India is that it is trapping young men and women who constitute the best human resource of the country.

In Chapter One there is a preview of the drug scene as it operates in India. It highlights the problem of drug abuse as it has been emerging in India over the decades and also provides the perspective against which the challenges that lie ahead have to be faced. This chapter also reviews the relevant literature that could be usefully referred to for any further studies. The common key concepts relating to drug-behaviour have also been defined in this chapter.

Chapter Two details the various geographical drug routes that operate through India. It presents the *modus operandi* of the highly organised mafias working along Indian borders in the north-west and also in the eastern sector.

Chapter Three moves on to drug trafficking across international borders. It provides description of vulnerable countries in the drug trade with special reference to Africa, America, Asia and Oceania.

Drug is now a very widely used term. It includes a number of products. These have local names and one also referred to by slangs. Chapter Four deals with the types of drugs commonly used, their effects and withdrawal symptoms. Familiarity with the names and symptoms is basic to any measures to prevent and control the use of narcotics and psychotropic substances. The chapter also provides hints on how to identify a drug-user even in the initial stages.

Drug abuse is both the cause and effect of a number of social factors. Chapter Five deals with the socio-economic causes that are contributory and lead to drug abuse.

The existing social scene has been analysed with a view to identify some of the social evils and current practices that directly or indirectly prompt young men and women to take recourse to drugs. The special role of family has been discussed at length as this is one institution that is undergoing rapid structural changes, often for the worse.

Why is it that, placed under similar circumstances, some people are tempted to fall into the drug net while many others manage to keep off the temptation ? Chapter Six deals with the psychological correlates of drug abuse. The various personality types and provocations that influence a person's susceptibility have been discussed along with perceived effects sought by those taking recourse to drugs.

Having known all about the personality types most prone to drug abuse, the focus shifts to measures needed for prevention of drug abuse. Prevention models have been outlined in the Seventh Chapter. The models include those suitable for family, community and the workplace with special reference to colleges and universities.

In spite of all preventive measures being taken, there would still be cases of drug abusers and addicts in a society open to social cross-currents. Chapter Eight deals with various therapeutic strategies for treatment of drug addicts. Since individual's personality plays a key role in making him a drug abuser, there is description of the various psychological techniques that could help in bringing the drug abusers and addicts back into the mainstream of a drug-free life. Various medical treatments available for treatment of drug addiction have also been mentioned herein.

Chapter Nine attempts to explain why in spite of best efforts some de-addicted drug users revert to their original condition. Strategies for prevention of relapse have also been discussed.

Life Skill Training in terms of Self-Help Techniques find description in the Tenth Chapter. External help has a role in de-addiction but much more may be done by the addict on his own. He has to have a positive attitude and some clear goals to work for. Addiction to work for a goal can be the best disinfectant against drug abuse. The role of support systems and physical fitness have been outlined as effective measures for coping with distress.

Having established the need for prevention and described treatment strategies, Chapter Eleven passes over to practical difficulties involved in the implementation of drug control programmes. It highlights the efforts being made at international level to cope with these difficulties.

Chapters Twelve and Thirteen relate to the findings of studies made by the author while working as Psychologist attached to the Delhi University Guidance Bureau. Chapter Twelve is devoted to the findings recorded in the sample study.

Chapter Thirteen deals with the self-esteem structure of drug abusers as revealed in the investigative study for the same group. The emerging conclusions from chapters Twelve and Thirteen are pointers to the changing attitudinal structure among college-going young men and women of today.

Chapter Fourteen is devoted to the problems of the soft targets – the women and the street children. They need special care and protection in programmes of drug control and prevention of drug abuse. The chapter describes what is being done by international agencies and what needs to be done by individual societies.

There are a number of myths and false beliefs relating to drugs. The abusers frequently quote them to rationalise their behaviour. Chapter fifteen deals with some of these myths and explains how false and deceptive they are.

The last chapter concludes what needs to be done by various sectors of human society specially in India if we want a drug-free social order. The strength and weakness of the existing social system have been analysed and suggestions are made to achieve the goal of a drug-free India.

1

Drug Menace

The Indian Scene

Alcoholism and drug abuse, in their present form, are an alien concept so far as India and other similarly placed developing countries of the world are concerned. The tribal societies used to have a round of locally brewed drinks on festive occasions. Drugs like *bhang* were not unknown in India but their use was restricted to a very microscopic minority. These substances were never regarded as the 'in thing'.

In the highly developed societies, a stage came when the young were able to experience most of the pleasures at a very early age and started suffering from 'the frustration of achievement'. They started looking for the exotic realm of feelings and fascinating hallucinogenic experiences beyond the ordinary joys afforded by simple things of life. The use of alcohol and drugs got glamourised and attracted the attention of the youth whose counterparts in developing societies had to struggle for sheer existence.

The desperation to 'belong' is universal. The techno-societies, being complex, do not offer the individuals enough scope to maintain a sense of identity. The situation drives them to plug into one or more social sub-cults. As societies move up, the frustrations of the individuals also multiply. One starts looking for a cult wherein these frustrations could at least be consolidated, if not relieved. Sometimes one feels that the answer to all these lies in the use of drugs. It may be a case of super-simplification for coping with overload of stresses. In this process, it does not matter that the incredibly intricate human machine that God alone could have created grinds to a halt as more and more sand is poured in the locomotive.

There are around 4000 plants that yield substances capable of relieving pain and curing various diseases. These substances also yield pleasurable sensations when used by persons who are not sick. There are about 60 drugs derived from plants that have been used to get pleasurable sensations.

Psychotropic substances started getting abused around the sixteenth century when major socio-cultural changes started taking place in Western societies. Increasing urbanisation accelerated the process with which drug-using behaviour spread over large parts of population. The traditional and ritualised societies had built-in checks against deviant behaviour. Complex and free societies loosened these checks leading to greater use of drugs.

The geographic alienation was broken as more and more ships sailed from Europe to Asian and African countries. The drug-using customs which were hitherto localised and restrained spread to other societies where there were no customary checks on their consumption. Technological developments like establishment of distilleries made the task much simpler as the locally brewed alcoholic drinks were crude and took time for preparation. Heroin and crack emerged on the scene as an outcome of the technological sophistications. European nations developed commercial interest in the sale of opium to countries like China. The Western nations could have never visualised a scenario that while the Chinese would get off the hook, future generations in their own countries would make drug-addiction a global problem. The 'hippie' cult is a typical example of the backlash.

The cult of 'hippies' which believed in free sex and love evolved at Height Ashbury as an escape from the realities of life. They introduced L.S.D. and other drugs as a 'mind-expanding' source. By 1969, Height Ashbury was dissolved and hippies were banned in a number of countries. However, they continued to haunt countries like India where drugs like hemp and cannabis were more freely available and also because they found acceptance among the youth, specially in elite schools and colleges.

Alcoholism and drug abuse have been spreading their tentacles in the Indian cities and towns at an alarming rate. Some idea of the incidence can be had from the special reports available in respect of select Indian cities.

Puri is one of the four dhams, the sacred places of India. It is the abode of Lord Jagannath and attracts pilgrims from all parts of the country. It has also become notorious for the easy supply of drugs like ganja, charas, opium and brown sugar. While the police and the administration adopt an ostrich-like approach to the menace, addicts can be seen spread over the beach in large numbers. The locals accept that during the worship of Trinath (Brahma the creator, Vishnu the sustainer and Mahesh the destroyer), bhang is freely distributed irrespective of the age and sex of the pilgrims. Ganja is a sanctified offering to the Lord. It is also inhaled as 'prasad' through a clay pipe 'chilam' by all present.

The most unfortunate and surprising part of the findings of a recently conducted survey in this town (1990) is that over 60 per cent young addicts accepted that they were first initiated into the drug by their parents. With increase in the number of addicts, more and more varieties of drugs are becoming available in the holy city.

The Malwa region comprising Faridkot, Bhatinda, Mansa, Sangrur and Sirsa is a recent addition to the drug prevalent areas in northern India. Formerly people in the area restricted themselves to the use of country-made liquor and opium husk. These were available from licensed dealers and their use was confined to adults. Opium addicts were hardly one or two per village. The situation has changed radically. The drugs now consumed in the Malwa region include morphine, diazepam, carrisoma tablets, codine, corex, phenysedyl and brown sugar. The consumption runs into crores of rupees every year. There has been a very significant increase in the number of heroin addicts. Intravenous drugs are being consumed by three to four times more people as compared to figures four years back.

Drug abuse studies conducted at the PGI, Chandigarh, have revealed that drug abuse ranged from casual to regular, to lifetime to lifetime regular. The highest increase (62%) was registered in the category lifetime use. Chandigarh and Bhatinda have de-addiction centres where over 5,000 addicts were registered during 1993 – 94. These included over 2,000 poppy husk addicts and another over 1,000 opium addicts. Unfortunately the number of addicts from the poorer sections of the society was found to be three times as compared to those from the upper strata of the society.

The worst affected are the North Eastern States of Manipur and Nagaland. The number of addicts in Manipur alone is estimated to be around 40,000. Almost every family in Imphal and Churachandpur has one member, invariably a youth, hooked onto heroin. Jails in Imphal are reported to be full of addicts with many parents preferring to send them there to prevent havoc at home. Most addicts take drugs intravenously causing a major AIDS threat in the region.

Studies conducted on Bombay city show that drug addiction has been claiming on an average five lives everyday. The Bombay police Narcotics Cell reports (1994), "The city is worst affected as far as drugs are concerned, with brown sugar most popular among addicts."

In Cochin, brown sugar has begun to make deep inroads into the city youth. The police chief says, "There is every possibility of Cochin becoming a drug nerve-centre" (1994).

Ahmedabad, Surat, Baroda and Rajkot are the places in Gujarat where smack and hashish are consumed on a large scale. The DCP, Ahmedabad, reports, "The majority of petty criminals are hardcore addicts who steal to support their habit."

The extent of drug addiction among students in medical colleges was assessed in Agra (U.P.) and Madras. It was found that in case of Agra, 56 per cent students were drug addicts (74 per cent men and 57 per cent women). The Madras study found 35 per cent medical students as being drug addicts. Majority of the addicts lived in hostels.

There has been an alarming increase in the number of female drug addicts. The number of female drug addicts has been on the increase in colleges and universities. In a survey conducted by the Indian Council of Medical Research (1988), it was revealed that one-fourth of the students at Allahabad University were drug addicts, the girls outnumbering the boys. Both sections of students at Varanasi had tasted opium, alcohol, cannabis, cocaine, heroin, L.S.D. pathedine, morphine and anti-pregnancy drugs more than once. The students of Bombay were found to have used drugs frequently. The girls among the frequent users comprised 55 per cent of the surveyed population.

Surprisingly, even the lady doctors, well aware of the consequences of the abuse, have exhibited their interest in drug-use. An in-house study conducted by the Department of Psychiatry of the Madras Medical College revealed that 20 per cent female interns took alcohol regularly. But more alarming was the fact that over 25 per cent of the boys and 35 per cent of the girls were hooked to drugs like cannabis. It is noteworthy that due to the physiological formations, girls take only six years to get completely addicted while the boys take upto ten years. Added to it is the unfortunate situation that girls rarely report to de-addiction clinics because of prevalent social taboos.

A Commonwealth-sponsored study on 'Women, their families and drugs' conducted in Calcutta in the '90s revealed that out of the total addicts in the city, 4 per cent were women, mostly hailing from high or upper middle class families. The average age of addicts was 27 for heroin users and 35 for the alcoholics. The minimum age for the heroin addicts was 16. About 60 per cent of women addicts were married. About 46.67 per cent earned a salary below Rs. 2000 per month.

Drug addiction has spread even among the school-going girls in Aizawl (Manipur). The available figures for 1994 revealed that among the 933 drug addicts, there were at least 81 girls. Drug abusers there have been found getting hooked to proxyvon which is medicinally used as a pain-killer. Other alternatives include nitrosun, diazepam, socygon and morphine.

A Delhi-based survey had revealed that among adolescent heroin users, school students comprise 34.48 per cent of the addict population.

The drug menace is not confined to regular school or college students. The menace has its victims among street children too. *Patriot* (March 28, 1993) reported that 100 million street children have taken to drugs as per WHO estimates. Most children use alcohol, hashish, solvents and medicines that are both cheap and easily available.

The accessibility of drugs was at one time a difficult problem. The situation has changed radically and availability seems to have become as easy as getting a lollipop. Besides regular drug peddlers, there is the corner panwala, the milk vendor, the ward boy in the hospital, foreign tourists and students, refugees, waiters and even owners in restaurants, taxi or scooter drivers. All are willing to make a fast buck by peddling drugs in addition to their normal profession or vocation. Drug points have developed even in rural areas. Politicians and the police provide patronage to these peddlers about whom everyone in the college or university is well informed.

In New Delhi the region Pahargunj adjoining the New Delhi railway station has come up on the world map so far as illicit sale of narcotics is concerned. Nearly every house in the locality has turned into a guest house. Drug peddling is as common here as the sale of cigarettes or eatables.

In Delhi, drug peddling business involves restaurant owners, juice wallas, pan-shops, scooter-rickshaw drivers and university students. The areas around Delhi School of Economics, a place adjacent to the church near the Reeds line, college hostels, and some *dhabas* and tea stalls in the North Campus have been identified as drug outlets.

Drug peddling shops are so well known that one hardly has to make an effort to find them. There are joints at Yusuf Sarai, near IIT, and Jia Sarai, their patrons being students from JNU and AIIMS besides the IIT. Mohan Singh Place and Palika Bazar too have shops peddling in drugs and the addicts know them. At the Majnu ka Tila, the Tibetan chang is freely available. The nerve-centre of the metropolis is Palam. Mehrauli with its dense foliage has cafes where the junkies sit and share 'chilum'.

The Hindustan Times (June 1994) report made some startling revelations about the drug trade in Delhi. It revealed that Delhi's drug den lies in the Yamuna Pushta JJ (Jhuggi-Jhonpri) colony. The entrance to this lies through a big hole in the inner wall of the Nigambodh burning ghat. One goes through a series of concrete pipes to reach a cluster of hutments. There in an open space, one finds men, women and even children scattered fixing themselves with 'brown sugar'.

The addicts are chronic cases of addiction who have given up any hope of redemption. Just by their side lies human refuse with flies alternating between their faces and the defecations. The sight is too ghastly and even frightening.

The addicts include both the former traffickers and the outsiders. There are students, retired police officials, transport workers, destitutes and a large number of rag-pickers.

The slum area has cottages where the process of adulterating and repacking goes on with the efficiency of a cottage industry. An average packer makes Rs. 100 per day. There are around 2000 persons involved in the illicit trade in this area. The average daily sale is estimated to be around Rs. 2.5 to 3 lakhs.

New centres are developing as the city expands. The latest in the list is the JJ Colony in West Delhi (Sagarpur-Dabri).

In Bombay, drug-peddlers operate around schools and colleges in the guise of *panwallas* or *chanawallas*. Initially the children are offered a puff free. Later the cigarettes are loaded and sold on credit. Once trapped, the supply is stopped till the payment has been made. The areas where brown sugar and drugs are peddled include Colaba, Bandra, Dongri, Pydhonie and Nagpada.

In Calcutta,the gaining grounds for drugs are Kalitala in Dhakuria, Golpark in South Calcutta and Sudder Street where supply is smooth and varied but the guest houses caution in bold prints 'No Dope Allowed'.

Young people's parties are no longer complete without disco music and drugs. In the important colleges, the addicts have become cult figures. Hostels abound with students who live on methaquanol tablets. Ganja is available in almost every slum or roadside settlement. Heroin is available in Teritti Bazar. The Chinese dealing in heroin goes even to the extent of getting the addicts to mental hospitals when they lose consciousness.

In Manipur 'Number Four' is the name for heroin and even school-children know it. The average age of initiation here is 12 years, the maximum concentration of the users being in the 14-25 age group.

In Srinagar, consumption of brown sugar is spreading in almost all the localities. Houseboats, hostels and tabas in Srinagar are becoming peddlers' paradise in increasing numbers.

Heroin addiction is no longer confined to metropolitan or big cities. It has spread to cities like Madurai, Bangalore etc. Smack has spread its tentacles to small places and suburbs like Palwal (Haryana), Ghaziabad (U.P.) and areas near the metropolitan cities such as Sonepat or Bahadurgarh.

According to UN Narcotics Control Strategy Report of February, 1993, there are about one million heroin addicts and four million opium addicts in India. Nearly 13,000 people were booked for drug trafficking in 1992 which was more than twice the figure of 1989. Till July, 1993, 3,707 persons including 42 foreign nationals had been arrested as per report of the Narcotics Control Board.

Drug abuse has shown a quantum jump. While 16,000 people were registered with the Central De-addiction Centres in 1986-87, their number had shot up to 97,000 in 1991-92 over six times increase.

The Ministry of Social Welfare, Government of India, had recorded 8,11,592 drug addicts till December, 1992. The statistics was confined to those who had registered themselves with some clinics or de-addiction centres. The unreported cases would be many times the recorded figure. The position is gradually becoming alarming.

The National Master Plan for Drug Abuse Control 1994-2000 states that urban slum population and youth, mostly in the 16-25 age group, are highly vulnerable to drug abuse. It adds that 1,459,512 urban marginal workers, 58,171,890 urban male non-workers and 36,931,000 unemployed job-seekers in the country constitute the most susceptible segment.

WHO had estimated nearly 50 million as the number of addicts in the world as far as 1985. Of them 30 million used marijuana, 8 million were addicted to cocaine, 1.7 million were the opium addicts, 70,000 used heroin and the rest used other drugs. The problem has since assumed manifold increase both in the number of addicts and the countries involved. International mafias controlling the illicit drugs make profits running into hundreds of billions of dollars.

Twenty-five years back, drug addiction was only a problem but not a menace in India. Today the abuse has assumed frightening dimensions. Caught in the net are young men and women, both educated and uneducated, artists, artisans, labourers, jilted lovers, film stars, businessmen and even the elite sections of society.

A sustained war on drug abuse has to be launched before it becomes too late. During the years 1990-95 the UN funded to the extent of $ 400 million for combating the drug menace. The government needs to mobilise its resources to create an effective and adequate infrastructure. India has to take a lesson from USA. The people in USA seem to have accepted that it is now impossible to beat drug abuse. They have started debating whether it would be alright if the use of drugs was legalised. Fortunately for India and similarly-placed developing countries the situation is not so bad. The time to act is now before the matter assumes dimensions that the Government of India may find it near-impossible to control with its meagre resources and a work culture in which everything goes.

Definitions of commonly used terms

Drug Abuse : Use of a drug for purposes other than medicinal.

Psychological Dependence : The compulsion to continue a drug despite its untoward consequences.

Physical Dependence : Specific syndrome of physical symptoms upon abrupt withdrawal of a drug.

Drug Tolerance : The declining effect upon administration of a given dose of a drug.

Cross Tolerance : Use of one drug inducing tolerance to another drug of the same class.

Drug Misuse : Indiscreet administration of drugs by physicians.

Drug Addiction : An expert committee on drugs (WHO, 1950) defined drug addiction as "a state of periodic or chronic intoxication detrimental to the individual and to the society, produced by the repeated consumption of a drug natural or synthetic". Symptoms of drug addiction are a desire and compulsion to continue, to increase the dose of the drug and psychic dependence.

Drug Habitation : "A condition resulting from the repeated consumption of the drug." Its symptoms are desire (not compulsion) to continue, no tendency to increase the dose, some degree of psychological dependence but absence of physical dependence.

Gateway Drugs : Soft drugs lead to other strong drugs. The soft drugs are termed as gateway drugs. Alcohol, tobacco, marijuana etc. are a few examples of gateway drugs. Dr. Robert L. Dupont mentions in "Getting Tough on Gateway Drugs" that 12 to 17 years old who are smokers are twice as likely to be current users of alcohol as are non-smokers and 14 times are likely to use cocaine, heroin or hallucinogens. The studies of Johnston O'Malley and Bachman (1975-86) show an association between smoking, alcohol and drug use.

2

India in the Drugs Conduit

It is estimated that about three-fourth of the heroin produced out of illicit poppy that finds its way into India is grown in the Golden Crescent — Pakistan, Afghanistan and Iran. The drug mafia has its tentacles spread out from Kashmir to the north-eastern regions as also on the high seas off the metropolitan ports of Bombay and Madras. The mafia hold is becoming stronger day-by-day.

Geographically, India has a number of soft borders. Due to these borders, India is emerging as a transit country for drug trafficking. The political upheavals in Afghanistan have played a major role in drug peddlers settling down along the Pakistan-India border and from there into Rajasthan and Punjab through the soft border. A new narcotic route has emerged with Bombay as the transit point for opium-based drugs originating from north-west Pakistan and destined for Europe and the USA. Raw opium grown in Afghanistan finds its way into Pakistan where it is converted into heroin for onward transmission and use.

The smuggling of heroin and hashish is carried on through a vicious combination comprising smugglers and terrorists. Punjab and Jammu and Kashmir have borders with Pakistan that are easily negotiable for the smugglers. The terrorists join them with all the support that they get from across the Indian border. The Rajasthan sector also has a border with Pakistan. This sector is becoming increasingly vulnerable. There is over 1000 km. long border which cannot be fenced for geographical reasons. Drugs are popular with people on both sides of the border. Many families spread over both sides of the border find drug trafficking easy and highly lucrative in a terrain which otherwise offers little scope for honest occupations.

Jaisalmer and Barmer districts of Rajasthan are the two areas that pose a great threat to the country by way of trade in smuggled heroin. There are remote villages in these districts that are not easily accessible and where ordinary enforcement agencies cannot outwit the traditional smugglers who are much better equipped with information about the terrain and also have a much better capacity to survive the heat and sand.

The drug lords of Europe and America procure heroin from their contacts in India through their agents based in Lagos or Lusaka. The Bombay contact in turn procures the desired quantity from his counterpart in Pakistan.

In Pakistan, heroin is procured from crude laboratories that exist in the remote villages of NWFP. Similar laboratories also exist in areas of Afghanistan lying on the Pakistan border. Camel-loads of heroin then travel to Indian borders and cross during dark nights. In this operation 'crossing', the couriers make good commission. Their knowledge of the terrain and movements of the Border Security Force come handy to the drug lords. Usually one crossing covers upto 50 kg of heroin loaded on two and three camels. Besides heroin, the camelloads also include upto 20 kg of hashish packed in cassette shaped parcels.

It is not that there are no monitoring agencies on the border. But the native couriers cleverly monitor their movements. Once inside the Indian border, the illicit cargo is dumped at some easily identifiable sand dune. The couriers do not always accompany the camels. The camels have a high instinct to reach their homes across the desert. So, if an India-based camel is loaded and put across the Indian border, it would reach its home village along with its load even unescorted. This operation makes the couriers immune from the net of the monitoring agencies and the Border Security Force. The smuggled heroins have their own brands. The more popular ones are named '777', '555', Gul Nargis and Scorpio. Similarly, hashish goes by the name of 'Taj'. On the Indian side, Jodhpur has acquired notoriety for being the trafficking haven. The traffickers based there are informed about the arrival of the consignment and the sand dune is identified by the border outpost number. The dumped consignment is lifted and loaded into jeeps and other vehicles fitted with high speed and powerful engines. From the border post, the drugs now come to Jodhpur. The next destination is Kandla/Bombay. The highway connecting Bombay with Amritsar passes through Jodhpur and the jeeps and jongas loaded with the illicit drugs move on this very notorious track. Repacking is done at Bombay which is the exit point so far as India is concerned. Both ships and aeroplanes take the illicit cargo out of India. There are well-knit cartels with wings in India and Pakistan that look after the entire operation.

Yet another exit point is Delhi. Here also, the heroin comes via Rajasthan. It comes concealed in truckloads and railway parcels. Couriers carry illicit traffic from Delhi to outside India by air. Part of the heroin goes out concealed in air cargo. While heroin comes to India from Pakistan, India illegally exports acetic anhydride which is used in the manufacture of heroin in the crude laboratories situated in Pakistan. The liquid goes out in jerry cans loaded on camels. On the Indian side, the states of Gujarat, Maharashtra and Uttar Pradesh have acquired notoriety for manufacture of acetic anhydride for illicit export to Pakistan.

India's border with Pakistan is unfenced in the Rajasthan sector. The Punjab border is fenced but that hardly makes any perceptible difference so far as the extent of drug smuggling is concerned. Pakistani counterparts frequently toss over the packets across the fence. The packets are picked up by the Indian members of the drug cartel. Drugs also enter India from Pakistan by the rail service *via* Attari near Amritsar which is the last station on the Indian border.

Jammu and Kashmir is now the new haven for drug smugglers. The consignments come from Rawalpindi, Sialkot and Islamabad. The Indian points are Rajouri and Jammu. Further distribution takes place from Srinagar where Indian control is minimal for reasons of terrorist infiltration.

The Gujarat border, specially the Rann of Kutch, is another smuggling point. Small fishing boats fetch consignments from Karachi and unload them on the coast of Gujarat. Drug consignments delivered at Gujarat are redirected to Bombay. Ahmedabad and Kandla Port also handle the illicit drugs. Drug smuggling is often combined with smuggling of gold and silver. The bigger drug cartels handle drugs for exports and gold and silver as imports. Most cartels are owned by persons who have easy connections with overseas countries.

The vigil on smuggling through air traffic has become strict over the years. By sea, however, the smugglers beat the monitoring agencies by employing high-speed boats that carry drugs to ships waiting on the high seas.

Tourists from a number of African countries have been found frequently indulging in smuggling activities. They serve as couriers, often carrying heroin in small capsules in their stomach or rectum.

The market seems inexhaustible. There are new products and new markets evolving in a manner that would be the envy of traditional multinationals. The latest addition to illicit exports from India is 'methaqualone'. Manufactured in and around Bombay and in some parts of Gujarat, it has found a ready market in South Africa. The increasing illicit manufacture of methaqualone constitutes a major problem in India. Three clandestine units were dismantled in the Bombay area in 1992. The bulk of the methaqualone smuggled out of India in large quantities is destined for South Africa, but methaqualone abuse has also started to spread in African countries that are used as transit points. In January 1993, Indian authorities seized 3,200 kg of methaqualone bound for South Africa, their largest seizure to date.

Narcotic seizures are a frequent phenomenon. The consignments seized value Rs. 50 crores or even more in international markets. In the north-east, Silchar has become the distribution point. Situated in Assam, it links operations in heroin smuggling to Imphal in Manipur and Aizawl in Mizoram. From Myanmar, the heroin (about 20 kg. everyday) comes to India and passes on to Bangladesh. Bangladesh is the exit point to countries of the West. The drug smuggled in the north-eastern region from Myanmar is being consumed locally in large quantities. These drug addicts are soft targets for terrorist organisations that are now posing serious risk to national security.

Terrorist outfits in India recycle the sale proceeds for procurement of illicit arms, making the terrorist groups in Myanmar as well as in the north-eastern states of India self-sufficient in their needs for arms and ammunition. The situation needs strict monitoring.

Laos, Thailand and Myanmar constitute the golden triangle. It is the largest poppy growing area in the world accounting for production of over 2,000 tonnes of opium per year. East Myanmar is the major source of drugs in the golden triangle and to some extent drug smugglers have covert official patronage. Drug enforcement agencies estimate that Myanmar alone produces about 60 per cent of heroin of which 95 per cent goes to Europe and U.S.A. via Thailand and the rest via India. Heroin from the golden triangle is regarded as the purest available. It has a very high morphine content and is most sought after by addicts who take intravenous injections.

Nepal is another country on the drug traffickers' list. London, Paris and a number of European cities get their supplies via Nepal. The highest priced destination is New York. The prevailing price could be Rs. 10 million for a kilogram. The drug lords controlling most poppy cultivation and the refineries have recently been shifting their operational bases to the western regions of Myanmar. That makes things yet more difficult for India since the labs and refineries would now be yet nearer to the Indian border. Inside the Indian border, laboratories exist in Manipur. These labs are the major source of supply to the north-eastern states.

As in the case of the western regions, north-east exports acetic anhydride to labs situated across the Indian border in Myanmar.

Illicit drug traffic entering from Myanmar touches Moreh on the Indian border and moves on to Imphal for distribution. Recent disturbances caused by Kuki-Naga clashes led to the diversion of drug traffic from Moreh in Manipur to Champhai in Mizoram. The movement of drugs is facilitated by the terrain which is inhospitable for monitoring agencies. The local tribal population can move freely across the international border without any passport or *visa* restrictions. Originally this agreement had been reached to ensure easy supply of essential goods to the tribals through barter. Now it is misused both by genuine tribals and other couriers posing as tribals exempted from passport and *visa* restrictions. Many of them have established themselves in the illegal trade.

The couriers carry small amounts on their person as there are poor transport and communication facilities along the border. Within the Indian borders, the heroin finds its way to major consumption centres like Imphal, Kohima, Aizawl, Dibrugarh, Guwahati, Shillong, Agartala and Siliguri. The network, thus, extends to all the States of the north-east, Manipur, Nagaland, Mizoram, Assam, Meghalaya, Tripura down to the streets of Calcutta. The bordering areas of Mizoram, Manipur and Arunachal Pradesh have of late started growing poppy illegally. Thick jungles in Manipur offer safe places for poppy cultivation for which there is a ready and lucrative market.

The main entry point in India is Manipur from where the drugs go to Bangladesh via Assam and Tripura. Guwahati and Cachar have been the sites of many seizures. From Cachar, the drug consignments enter Tripura and go over to Chittagong hill tracts in Bangladesh and the Chittagong port for onward shipment. Upto the year 1993 Myanmar was producing about a thousand tons of heroin. The production is likely to go up to about 2,750 tonnes as the military junta in that country is not interested in curbing drug running. Fourteen refineries have been set up on the Myanmar-Manipur border. Myanmar government gave general amnesty to drug dealers to launder black money. This measure, which shocked American enforcement agencies, is believed to have netted for the government some $ 960 million.

Indian enforcement agencies have so far been concentrating on the western border. Only recently have they turned their attention to the north-east border as some members of the military and para-military forces deployed in the region for law and order duties were arrested while acting as couriers. In India, opium poppy is cultivated illicitly but opium is produced under government control. In 1992, some illicit poppy plantations were detected and eradicated in Arunachal Pradesh, Manipur and Rajasthan. More than 1.5 tonnes of opium was seized in India in the first six months of 1993. Illicit poppy plantations were also discovered in Nepal near the Indian border in 1992.

Clandestine heroin laboratories have been dismantled in Uttar Pradesh and in the border areas of Madhya Pradesh and Rajasthan. Large quantities of acetic anhydride have been seized in Gujarat and at the Indian border with Pakistan. Acetic anhydride has been placed under the control regime of the Narcotic Drugs and Psychotropic Substances Act by the Narcotic Drugs and Psychotropic Substances (Regulation of Controlled Substances) Order. The order, which came into force on 15 April, 1993, enhances controls over the manufacture, sale, import, export and transportation of acetic anhydride. About 16,000 litres of acetic anhydride were confiscated in the first six months of 1993.

Transit traffic in heroin from South-West and South-East Asia constitutes a major problem. Heroin seizures almost doubled in 1992 compared with figures for 1991 and the trend continued in 1993.

Manipur has also acquired notoriety for cultivation of cannabis. The area is very difficult to reach in most cases. The growers enjoy the protection of militants for a consideration. Ganja is also being cultivated in the State with protection being afforded by highly placed people. Bihar is a ready market for ganja. There have been cases where even the army personnel were found involved in the illicit carrying of ganja. There could be no worse situation for narcotics control agencies. Illicit cannabis plantations were destroyed in 1992 in Kerala, Manipur, Nagaland and Tamil Nadu. A significant increase in the illicit cannabis traffic has, however, been observed by the Indian authorities; 50 tonnes of cannabis and large illicit consignments of cannabis resin were seized in India along its borders with Nepal and Pakistan in the first six months of 1993. Nepal remains an important source of cannabis resin for countries in Europe, as well as for India.

A drug baron once remarked that drugs are the Third World's atom bomb. Illicit drugs produced in the Third World countries do have the potential of causing destruction among the western societies the way the US atom bomb caused havoc in Asia (Japan). The unsaid part of the statement is that there is no safe delivery system for drugs. The countries through which the trail of death passes become victims of the menace as much as those who are intended to be corrupted for financial gains. This is a special lesson for India.

The increase in illicit traffic in heroin has been accompanied by its growing abuse in certain parts of the region. In India, heroin abuse remains a major concern. Originally confined to the north-eastern states and larger cities, the habit is now reaching other areas. Intravenous administration of heroin and the high incidence of human immunodeficiency virus (HIV) infection resulting from that form of abuse have become major problems in Bombay and other cities. The abuse of heroin remains a major problem in Nepal, mainly in the Kathmandu and Pokhara valleys. In Sri Lanka, heroin abuse is increasing; there are about 50,000 heroin abusers, according to government estimates. Heroin abuse has recently escalated drastically in Maldives; the proportion of abusers in the total population is estimated to be very high; most of them are at Malé, the capital. Although the number of heroin-dependent persons remains relatively small in Bangladesh, heroin abuse is increasing, mainly among young people, in urban slum areas. A recent study conducted in Dhaka has revealed that pethidine is being abused by students on a large scale. An increase in the incidence of buprenorphine abuse has been reported in India.

Drug production means more money and arms with the insurgents and terrorist groups undermining the authority and sovereignty of the State. It also threatens to tear apart the fragile social structure of the country already under severe strain due to problems like unemployment among the youth.

3

Drug Trafficking

The World Scene

The world as a whole is under the flanges of problems arising out of drug trafficking. Illicit drugs have become the world's most organised and high-profit industry. There are regular markets and supply lines that extend to all parts of the globe. The country-wise information available from the Report of the International Narcotics Control Board for 1993 is a comprehensive document from which relevant extracts are being reproduced to give an overall picture of the problem.

AFRICA

Cannabis remains the most abused drug in Africa. In most countries in the region, illicit cannabis markets are supplied mainly by local cultivation and regional trafficking. In northern, western and central Africa, the main source countries seem to be, respectively, Morocco, Nigeria and Zaire. There are signs that cannabis cultivation is increasing throughout the region, mainly in Lesotho, Malawi, South Africa, Swaziland, Uganda and Zambia. That increase is connected with growing domestic demand with the stepped up activity of international illicit traffickers, who use the large-scale cannabis plantations as supply sources for the European market. Cannabis plantations cover more than 50,000 hectares in Morocco. According to government estimates, the country remains the main source of the cannabis resin found in European countries, but the increasing incidence of shipments and amounts of cannabis originating in western and central African countries is a clear indicator of an emerging trend. Seaports in northern and eastern Africa are often used as transit points for cannabis resin being transported from West Asia to Europe.

The abuse of cannabis is widespread in the region. Even without epidemiological studies, it can be stated that in some African countries cannabis abuse has become endemic. There has been a steady increase in the number of persons who abuse cannabis in combination with alcohol, pharmaceuticals (mainly psychotropic substances) and organic solvents. In addition to political and socio-economic conditions and war, limited law enforcement capabilities and prevention programmes have contributed to the increase in drug abuse. Besides cannabis, abuse of opiates is also common in several countries of Africa.

Illicit poppy cultivation has been reported only in Egypt and Kenya, but illicit traffic in and abuse of opiates (mainly heroin) has increased in several parts of the region. Airports in western Africa and several seaports in Africa have been used by international criminal organisations to transport heroin shipments from Asia. Nigerians, who are frequently used by such organisations as couriers to smuggle heroin into European countries, are reportedly being replaced, at least to some extent, by nationals of other countries in western Africa. The transit activity, which has recently been expanded to include airports in central and eastern Africa, has had a spillover effect on illicit markets in eastern, western and central Africa. A few years ago, the abuse of opiates in Africa as a whole was limited. Recently, however, the Governments of Burundi, Cameroon, Egypt, Kenya, Nigeria, Senegal, Swaziland, United Republic of Tanzania and Zambia have been increasingly reporting cases involving heroin abuse.

African transit routes and couriers from western Africa are increasingly being used by international criminal organisations to transport cocaine from South America to Europe. Despite a decrease in the amounts of cocaine seized in Africa, more and more countries are reporting illicit cocaine transactions on their territories.

Despite an increase in the number of cases involving the abuse of heroin and cocaine, the abuse of certain psychotropic substances and cannabis has generally remained a problem in the region. The abuse of stimulants, hypno-sedatives and anxiolytics (minor tranquillisers) has been reported in all of the sub-regions of Africa.

The clandestine manufacture of methamphetamine and amphetamine and of tablets containing them is limited to a few countries in northern and eastern Africa; the bulk of the amphetamine, pemoline and other stimulant tablets are smuggled into Africa, mainly out of Asia and

Europe. It is expected that the commitment of the Bulgarian authorities to stop the illicit manufacture and shipment of amphetamine and amphetamine-type stimulants will result in a discontinuation of the supply of those drugs from eastern Europe.

Barbiturates and benzodiazepines are abused throughout Africa. Secobarbital remains the most popular barbiturate, diazepam is the leading benzodiazepine tranquilliser and flunitrazepam (sold under the brand name rohypnol) is the most frequently reported benzodiazepine hypnotic; however, dozens of other brand names and generic forms of benzodiazepines are mentioned in many national reports.

South Africa has experienced a major drug problem since the 1970s, when the traditional but limited abuse of cannabis started to spread to all categories of the population. The large-scale abuse of illicit methaqualone later became a major problem. In South Africa, methaqualone is most commonly abused in conjunction with cannabis and smoked in a pipe.

Kenya had been considered a transit country used in the illicit traffic in methaqualone from India to South Africa. It has gradually become a country in which methaqualone is abused and has recently become an important illicit manufacturer of methaqualone. Clandestine laboratories for the illicit manufacture of methaqualone or methaqualone tablets have been detected by law enforcement authorities but law enforcement activities are hindered by the lack of adequate national legislation.

In its report for 1992, the Board* referred to certain problems connected with the illicit traffic in and abuse of khat (*catha edulis*). Khat trade and consumption are not prohibited or regulated by the international drug control treaties; however, several African countries have introduced measures prohibiting such activity in the region and some European countries have taken measures to prevent khat from being imported into their territories. There are reports that there are links between the trade in khat and the procurement of weapons in the Horn of Africa and that the use of khat (which is considered abuse in several African countries) is increasing. There are conflicting views concerning whether there is a need for the international community to take action against khat trade and consumption.

* International Narcotics Control Board

AMERICA

The situation in Central America and Caribbean is rather serious. Drug traffickers have continued to take advantage of the strategic position of the Caribbean sub-region to transship considerable quantities of cannabis and cocaine to North America and, to some extent, to Europe. There is also evidence that some heroin destined for those regions has been shipped across the chain of islands that make up the Caribbean. A number of States in the sub-region are experiencing downturns or stagnation in their economies. The concomitant rise in unemployment appears to have led to an increase in crime, much of which has been drug-related. In Barbados, for example, government officials have linked an increase in drug abuse and illicit trafficking to unprecedented growth in the crime rate, as well as a decline in the tourist industry, one of the cornerstones of the Barbadian economy.

Cannabis cultivation, mainly for local consumption, continues in the region. Cannabis cultivated in Jamaica continues to enter Canada and the United States. In Jamaica, most of the cannabis cultivation is now confined to small plots to reduce the possibility of detection. Cannabis smoking remains the most common form of drug abuse in the majority of the countries in the region.

There have been no reports on illicit drug manufacture but some clandestine laboratories for refining cocaine or converting cocaine hydrochloride into crack may exist. As a consequence of the large-scale transit activity, increasing cocaine abuse has been reported in several countries in Central America. The situation is similar in the Caribbean, where the abuse of crack has become more frequent. The number of drug-related deaths is on the increase in the Caribbean sub-region.

Despite existing legislation, the availability of sophisticated surveillance systems, and government efforts against illicit drug trafficking, Costa Rica lacks the human resources and equipment to effectively fight illicit drug trafficking and related crimes.

North America

In the United States, according to the 1992 National Household Survey on Drug Abuse, the number of abusers of any illicit drug continued to fall (in 1991, the figure was 12.6 million; in 1992, 11.4 million). There was, however, an increase of 7 per cent in the number of drug-related emergency cases, a development that was attributed to the increased purity of drugs (above all, heroin), increased potency (in the case of cannabis products) and more dangerous methods of administration. In Canada, overall drug abuse among youth has been declining; however, there has been an alarming increase in the abuse of volatile solvents, particularly gasoline, among young people in rural areas. Although volatile solvents are not subject to international control, the illicit demand for such substances reflects the general situation with regard to substances of abuse.

Substantial amounts of cannabis are smuggled into the United States out of Colombia, Jamaica and Mexico. However, domestic cultivation is becoming increasingly important as a source of supply for the illicit local cannabis market in the United States. Cannabis is increasingly being grown indoors in the United States; the latest developments in computer technology are being used to optimise growing conditions. In June, 1993, the average tetrahydrocannabinol (THC) content of normal "commercial grade" cannabis and of unpallinated and seedless female (sinsewilla) cannabis was 3.3 and 7.9 per cent, respectively, compared with less than 2 per cent and 6 per cent, respectively, in the late 1970s. In 1993, a sample from domestic cannabis seized at Washington D.C., was found to have a THC content of 30 per cent, the highest level ever recorded in the United States. The number of dismantled indoor cannabis-growing operations in the United States reached 3,849 in 1992, up from 2,848 in 1991. In 1992, 346 tonnes of cannabis were seized in the United States, compared with 226 tonnes in 1991; in addition, there was an unprecedented decrease in seizures of cannabis resin : 1,141 kg. in 1992, compared with 80,836 kg. in 1991. In 1992, assets totalling 69.2 million were seized in the United States in connection with illicit cannabis cultivation and trafficking. According to estimates of the Government, 6,500 tonnes of cannabis were made available on the illicit market in the United States in 1992. In Mexico, cannabis production increased in 1992 as a result of favourable growing conditions. The Mexican authorities eradicated 16,872 hectares of cannabis in 1992. Mexico has continued its war against drug trafficking; in the past four years, it has seized over 2,200 tonnes of cannabis. In Canada, cannabis resin seizures decreased considerably, from 74 tonnes in 1991 to 15 tonnes in 1992; at the same time, however, seizures of cannabis and cannabis oil increased from 7.5 tonnes and 409 kg., respectively, in 1991 to 13.7 tonnes and 501 kg. in 1992. Cannabis resin continues to be smuggled into North America via operations originating in West Asia.

Cannabis remains the most commonly abused drug in the North American region. In Canada, despite a decline of 10 per cent, cannabis in all its forms continues to be the most widely abused drug; the national annual prevalence of cannabis abuse was reported to be 5 per cent. In Mexico, the estimated number of cannabis abusers remained at the level of the 1991 estimate; however, the estimated number of frequent cannabis abusers increased by 35 per cent from 1991 to 1992. In the United States, cannabis abuse has continued to decline steadily (the number of cannabis abusers decreased by 8 per cent in 1992); however, cannabis remains the most commonly abused drug in that country.

Even though Mexico is a party to the 1961 Convention, the 1971 Convention and the 1988 Convention, heroin is illicitly produced in Mexico almost exclusively for smuggling into the United States; Mexican heroin accounted for approximately 23 per cent of the heroin found on the illicit market in the United States in 1992, down from over 33 per cent in 1988. Heroin from south-west and south-east Asia has continued to enter the United States in significant quantities; in addition, Colombian heroin is being increasingly smuggled into the country. Total heroin seizures in the United States in 1992 amounted to 1,214 kg., a slight decrease compared with the 1991 total of 1,374 kg. Canada has continued to be targeted by south-east Asian heroin traffickers and to some extent by those from western Africa, the latter viewing Canada as a convenient entry point to the United States heroin market. In 1992, 110 kg. of heroin were seized by the Canadian authorities.

Heroin abuse has remained a significant cause for concern in Canada and the United States, as street-level purity has increased and prices have decreased. In the United States, the number of heroin-related emergency cases increased by 16 per cent from 1991 to 1992. In Mexico, heroin abuse increased to some extent in 1992, when there were an estimated 17,000 heroin abusers in the country.

Cocaine, particularly crack, represents the primary challenge to drug law enforcement in the United States. These drugs are readily available in large quantities in virtually all major cities in the United States.

Colombian cartels have continued to send multi-kilogram cocainc shipments to North America. Increased amounts of cocaine have continued to be smuggled into Canada; in 1992, cocaine seizures totalled 5,202 kg., including a record seizure of 3,930 kg. that was made in Quebec. Mexican law enforcement authorities seized 38.8 tonnes of cocaine in 1992; it is estimated that 60 per cent of the cocaine entering the United States from Colombia passes through Mexico.

Although cocaine abuse has decreased among young people in middle-income suburban areas in the United States, hard-core drug abuse remains a serious problem, particularly among youth in lower-income, inner-city areas.

In 1992, 1,090 kg. of khat were seized in the United States. Khat is not under international control but substantial quantities of it have been seized in other parts of the world as well, mainly in Europe.

South America

In several South American countries, illicit drug production, manufacture, traffic and abuse are consequences and, at the same time, causes of fundamental economic and social problems.

Cannabis is cultivated in the majority of South American countries. In most countries, cannabis is being grown for local consumption but in some countries it is used to supply illicit markets in other countries. In Colombia, illicit cannabis plantations cover an estimated 7,000 hectares. In Brazil, 19.6 tonnes of cannabis were seized in 1992, compared with 8.5 tonnes in 1991. Cannabis smoking continues to pose a problem in most South American countries.

The raw cocaine base comprises coca paste. Peru remains the largest producer of coca leaf in the world. A fungus (*fusarium oxysporum*) has made coca bush cultivation less and less profitable in the Upper Huallaga valley. That, together with intensified interdiction operations, has resulted in coca bush growers moving northward to the Central and Lower Huallaga valleys, developing plantations there almost as fast as they are being wiped out in the south. The situation of drug law enforcement authorities is further complicated by the activities of terrorist movements. They are forced to fight not only illicit crop growers and traffickers, but also the guerrillas, a large portion of whose incomes forms 'war taxes' on illicit plantations and trafficking routes. Estimates on coca cultivation range from 130,000 to 350,000 hectares. Only a very small percentage of this cultivation is destined for licit purposes, into which the Peruvian law, contrary to the provisions of the 1961 Convention, includes coca chewing and the use of leaves for the manufacture of *mate de coca* (coca tea bags).

In Bolivia, approximately 40,000 hectares of land are under coca bush cultivation. Approximately one-third of the cultivation is considered to serve licit purposes. Some of these licit purposes, contrary to the provisions of the 1961 Convention, include coca chewing and the use of the leaves by a number of private companies, for the manufacture of *mate de coca* and a wide variety of products, the medical value of which has not yet been properly determined.

Coca bush cultivation continues in eastern Colombia, where plantations have been estimated to cover about 50,000 hectares. Coca bush cultivation is also taking place in Brazil, especially in the Amazon area.

Colombia remains the world's greatest supplier of cocaine hydrochloride, manufactured from coca paste (raw cocaine base) smuggled into Colombia, mainly out of Bolivia and Peru. Despite intensified law enforcement action, which led to the dismantling of 224 clandestine laboratories in 1992 and 109 in the first four months of 1993, the illicit manufacture of cocaine hydrochloride and *basuco* (unrefined cocaine base) continues to increase in eastern Colombia.

Colombian cartels have continued to expand their activities in a number of other countries. Venezuela, one of the countries that borders Colombia, has become a major transit country; traffickers there send tonnes of cocaine by ship to Europe and by aeroplane and by boat to the United States. Argentina, Brazil and Chile are also increasingly becoming important transit countries for illicit drug consignments destined not only for North America and Europe, but also for Asia and Africa. Almost all countries in South America are now increasingly being used for the transshipment of cocaine in other regions of the world. Governments in the region should pay attention to the possible increasing use of their free ports and free zones for illicit drug trafficking and should devise more efficient mechanisms for the monitoring of shipments, in line with the requirements of the international drug control treaties.

The abuse of amphetamines, anxiolytics and other pharmaceuticals has been reported in several South American countries. It is difficult to assess the magnitude of the problem, however, because of the deficiencies of most of the pharmaceutical control systems of the countries in the region. Despite adequate formal legislation, pharmaceuticals containing psychotropic substances are being dispensed without prescription in pharmacies and there are many loopholes in the pharmaceutical supply and distribution systems. The inspection of pharmacies is not adequately organised in many countries in the region, resulting in the dispensing of pharmaceutical preparations without the presence of a pharmacist. The situation is further complicated by the fact that many pharmaceutical products, including a large amount of counterfeit or fake products, are smuggled out of one country into another.

In South American countries, one of the greatest substance abuse problems remains the inhalation of organic solvents, a common habit of street children in urban slums. In Bolivia, Chile, Colombia, Ecuador and Peru, the abuse of inhalants, as well as coca paste, is prevalent among street children and causes irreversible health damage.

Colombia has a long history of violence and anti-government activities. Drug trafficking, however, is infiltrating legal business life, and drug traffickers are always trying to gain influence in the legislature and in the administration. Guerrilla-type associations and illicit drug cultivation and trafficking are closely linked.

Reports from Uruguay indicate that that country does not seem to be affected by drug abuse and illicit trafficking to the same extent as many other countries. The International Narcotics Control Board trusts that the competent authorities will remain vigilant in order to be able to react in a timely manner to the ever-changing drug abuse and illicit trafficking situation and to take suitable preventive measures. Uruguay seems to have been spared most major abuse problems; however, because of indiscriminate prescription of benzodiazepines in the country, its per capita consumption of such drugs is among the highest in the world.

Free ports and free trade zones of Uruguayan territory do not seem to be controlled in accordance with Article 18 of the 1988 Convention. Money-laundering is not yet a punishable offence. Uruguay has not become a party to the 1988 Convention. Such a situation might be used by trafficking organizations, which often shift their operations to those parts of a region where there is a minimum of risk. Therefore, the adoption of new laws and decrees taking fully into account the provisions of the 1988 Convention is a matter of urgency.

ASIA

East and South-east Asia

Large-scale cannabis plantations have been detected in the Laos People's Democratic Republic, Myanmar and Thailand. Increasing illicit traffic in cannabis has been reported in several areas in the region since 1992. The size of the cannabis consignments is also increasing, as demonstrated by a record seizure of 1,555 kg. in Hong Kong. Cannabis is the most abused drug in several countries in the region, including Indonesia, Malaysia and the Philippines, and an increase in the incidence of its abuse has been observed in Japan and the Republic of Korea.

South-east Asia continues to remain a major producer of illicit opium. Illicit opium poppy cultivation is mainly taking place in Myanmar, above all in the areas along its borders. In east Asia, increasing illicit opium poppy cultivation has been reported in the Republic of Korea, about 50,000 opium poppy plants were eradicated in the first half of 1993, compared with about 13,000 plants in the same period of 1992.

China (mainland and Taiwan province), Hong Kong, Japan, Malaysia, the Philippines, the Republic of Korea, Thailand and Vietnam are increasingly being used as transit points for illicit consignments of heroin from South-east Asia destined for Australia, Canada and the United States, as well as for countries in Europe. Bangkok remains an important embarkation point for heroin couriers bound for Europe and North America; in 1992, a total of 350 kg. of heroin was seized at the airport at Bangkok. In the first half of 1993, 1,945 kg. of opium and 1,898 kg. of heroin were seized by the Chinese authorities, mainly in Yunnan province, which is adjacent to the north-east border of Myanmar. In China, the growing frequency of seizures and amounts seized reflects the increasing illicit traffic and, at the same time, more effective law enforcement efforts. The number of officers of the Chinese drug law enforcement authorities (police and customs) has been substantially increased, their training has been improved and special anti-drug squads with drug-scenting dogs have been established.

A radical change has been reported in the Republic of Korea. Until 1992, the Republic of Korea had been used as a transit country for heroin from South-east Asia; but in 1992 and 1993, an unprecedented number of heroin abuse cases has been detected. Due to a similar spillover effect, Taiwan province of China also seems to be on its way to becoming an area in which heroin is abused.

The illicit manufacture of, traffic in and abuse of amphetamines, above all methamphetamine, constitute a major problem in several countries in the region. Taiwan province of China has remained a major supplier of methamphetamine for Japan, the Philippines and the Republic of Korea, but the illicit manufacture of the drug has also taken place in other areas.

West Asia

The cultivation of cannabis and the production of and illicit traffic in cannabis resin constitute a major problem in the region. There are indications that Afghanistan has remained the main source of cannabis resin that is smuggled into Pakistan to be transported to Europe along different trafficking routes. The cultivation of cannabis and the production of cannabis resin are also taking place on Pakistan territory, mainly in the North-West Frontier Province. The successful eradication campaigns conducted in 1991 and 1992 in the Beqaa valley in Lebanon have been continued in 1993. It was pointed out in the report of the Board for 1992 that cannabis grows wild on about 140,000 hectares in Kazakhstan and 6,000 hectares in Kyrgyzstan. There is considerable illicit traffic in cannabis in CIS member-States, moving from central Asia towards other parts of the former Union of Soviet Socialist Republics.

In Pakistan, 191 tonnes of cannabis resin were seized in 1992 by the law enforcement authorities. The variety of transit routes of countries in the region where substantial amounts of cannabis resin were seized in 1992 had been Iran, Jordan, Lebanon, Saudi Arabia, Turkey, United Arab Emirates and Yemen. Large quantities of cannabis resin destined for Europe are transported via seaports in Africa, mainly in eastern Africa. According to CCC reports, between May and September, 1993, nearly 25 tonnes of cannabis resin were seized in four European countries on their way through Africa in containerised shipments of either tea or cotton fabrics.

Afghanistan remains one of the largest producers of illicit opium in the world. According to some estimates, in 1992, poppy was cultivated on about 57,000 hectares and about 2,000 tonnes of raw opium were produced. Despite the recent use of satellite imagery, the lack of accurate data on illicit poppy cultivation and opium production in Afghanistan continues to pose a problem. In Pakistan, a rising trend in illicit poppy cultivation has been observed after an initial drop immediately after the ban entered into force in 1979. Enforcement of the ban is difficult because of the constitutional status of the tribal areas of the North-West Frontier Province, where most of the illicit poppy cultivation takes place. Opium production in Pakistan is estimated at 140-180 tonnes annually. The systematic large-scale eradication of illicit poppy plantations has continued in Lebanon.

Despite the ban on illicit opium production that was introduced in 1987 during the Soviet regime, such production continues in most newly independent States of the former Union of Soviet Socialist Republics. Farmers grow poppy on small plots and in gardens, mostly for their personal use. The eradication of a number of such poppy fields is regularly reported in Kazakhstan, Kyrgyzstan and Turkmenistan, but many, especially those in inaccessible mountainous areas, remain undetected.

Most of the processing of opium into heroin in Pakistan is believed to take place in the Tirah area of the Khyber district, close to the border with Afghanistan. It is difficult to control the so-called Durand line, the border between Afghanistan and Pakistan, which cuts through practically inaccessible tribal territories. Due to that situation, the drug problem of Pakistan is interconnected with that of Afghanistan. Around 100 heroin laboratories are believed to be operating in that area.

The illicit traffic in opium, morphine and heroin within the region and the smuggling of heroin out of the region into other regions, mainly Europe, remain major problems. Increased illicit trafficking in morphine and heroin has been reported in Jordan, Lebanon and the Syrian Arab Republic. In Yemen, two tonnes of morphine were seized in January, 1993 from a ship *en route* from Pakistan to Turkey.

About 154,000 Israelis are estimated to abuse psychoactive substances, including sleeping pills and methadone. Of the 30,000 people in that group who are considered to be drug-dependent, 60 per cent are heroin-dependent. Cannabis and heroin are the most popular drugs of abuse; the abuse of cocaine and hallucinogens is secondary, although increasing. Heroin is smoked rather than injected. Flunitrazepam and fenetylline are also abused, usually in combination with heroin. The abuse of cannabis resin, originating mostly in Lebanon, is widespread in Israel. In recent years, there has been a radical shift from cannabis resin to heroin.

EUROPE

Abolition of border controls within EEC, the opening of the borders between east and west and the political turmoil and open war in former republics of Yugoslavia constitute major challenges to drug control and law enforcement authorities in the fulfilment of their responsibilities.

The control of licit drug manufacture, trade and distribution has become complicated in formerly socialist countries in the region because of the huge number of new companies that have started to manufacture and deal in narcotic drugs, psychotropic substances and precursors.

In the former Union of Soviet Socialist Republics, international trade by road, rail and air is steadily growing with virtually no control mechanisms in place.

The rise in criminality in Belarus, the Russian Federation and Ukraine is associated with drug trafficking. In 1992 in Belarus, 618 gangs of criminals involved in drug-related crimes were discovered. In the same year, in the Russian Federation, 20 tonnes of narcotic drugs were seized and the number of drug-related crimes rose to more than 29,000. Drug traffickers from Belarus, the Russian Federation and Ukraine are expanding their operations, often via Poland, to countries in central and western Europe, having made Warsaw and Prague their principal bases for contacts with international drug traffickers from the west.

Cases involving illicit cannabis cultivation have been reported in several countries, but such activity is usually limited to small plots of land, gardens or greenhouses. There are only four countries in the region — Belarus, the Netherlands, the Russian Federation and Ukraine — where domestic cannabis cultivation plays a major part in supplying illicit markets at home and in neighbouring countries. In the former Union of Soviet Socialist Republics domestic cultivation constitutes the main supply source for cannabis abusers. Substantial quantities of cannabis and cannabis resin are smuggled into the Netherlands besides the extensive illicit cannabis cultivation in that country (300,000 cannabis plants were destroyed there in 1992).

Cannabis remains the main drug of abuse in Europe. No changes have been observed concerning the extent of cannabis abuse in Europe as a whole, with the exception of formerly socialist countries where cannabis abuse has been increasing. Whereas in the United States, the number of cannabis abusers has decreased in the last few years, no such trend has emerged in Europe although more and more Governments have taken a position against the liberalisation of cannabis smoking. Even experts who were inclined to exempt from narcotics control measures marijuana with a THC content of 1 or 2 per cent no longer regard as 'soft' drugs the cannabis varieties cultivated in the Netherlands, which may be ten times more potent. The Government of the Netherlands has to take the necessary measures to limit the cultivation of cannabis and the expansion of so-called coffee-shops, in which a person may purchase up to 30 grams of cannabis products.

A great number of illicit poppy plantations have been detected in Belarus, the Russian Federation and Ukraine. The cultivation of poppy for culinary purposes has been traditional in those countries; however, the use of poppy straw, a by-product of that activity, to prepare an abusable extract is a recent phenomenon. Farmers in the CIS member-States in Europe have resisted a total ban against poppy cultivation that was introduced in 1987. The situation is slightly different in other formerly socialist countries, where poppy cultivation has remained a licit activity. In some countries, various measures have been introduced to prevent poppy straw from becoming freely available. For example, in Poland, a licensing system has been introduced and a new poppy variety with a low morphine content has been developed.

In Eastern Europe there are a number of 'kitchen laboratories' in which abusers process poppy straw.

West Asia remains the main source of heroin destined for Europe (70-80 per cent of the heroin seized in Europe in 1992 originated in that region). Turkey remains the principal gateway for illicit heroin consignments. The turmoil in former republics of Yugoslavia and the opening of the borders of formerly socialist countries have contributed to a northward shifting of the traditional Balkan route

(Turkey-Bulgaria-Yugoslavia-Austria-Germany). Diversification of trafficking routes has been noted: South-West Asian heroin is being increasingly smuggled through CIS member-States. The Czech Republic, Hungary, Romania and Slovakia are increasingly being used as storage and transshipment points for illicit heroin consignments destined for western Europe. The smuggling of heroin via Greece and by ferry from there to Italy continues. The Russian Federation has also become a transit country used in smuggling heroin out of south-east and south-west Asia into Europe.

The abuse of heroin continues to be a major problem in many European countries. Poppy straw extract is increasingly being abused in central and eastern Europe. The abuse of opiates in combination with barbiturates or other sedatives is not a new practice, but new variations have been reported in Germany (the abuse of opiates combined with pentobarbital or flunitrazepam), in Poland (the abuse of poppy straw extract mixed with barbiturates) and in the United Kingdom (the abuse of opiates combined with temazepam). The abuse of synthetic opiates (methadone, fentanyl and methylfentanyl) has been reported in the Russian Federation. An increase in deaths related to the abuse of drugs has been reported in several countries in the region.

The illicit traffic in and abuse of cocaine are increasing in Europe even in the eastern part of the continent. Colombia is still the source of the overwhelming majority of the cocaine found on illicit markets in Europe. Because of their linguistic and cultural ties with South America, Portugal and Spain constitute important points of entry for South American drug cartels co-operating with European drug trafficking syndicates at the distribution level. The largest cocaine seizures have been made in Spain, but seaports and airports in Belgium and the Netherlands seem to be frequent targets of bulk shipments of cocaine from South America.

Airports in eastern and central European countries (more recent examples being the airports at Budapest and Sofia) are frequently being used as transit points by cocaine couriers arriving from South America who continue by train or by road to their destinations in western Europe. Significant cocaine seizures have recently been made at the airport at Bucharest. And there are indications that the airport at Prague is being used as a transshipment point by South American cocaine traffickers operating with Czech nationals. In 1993, over 1 tonne of cocaine destined for illicit markets in western Europe was seized at St. Petersburg after it had been transported from Colombia by ship through Finland and Sweden. That seizure might indicate the opening of a new trafficking route.

OCEANA

Although the region has not yet become a focus of major international concern, the Pacific islands are increasingly being used by drug traffickers as transit points. The capacity of police and customs services is not sufficient to control the increasing illicit drug trade. In the region as a whole, with the exception of Australia and New Zealand, the problem of drug abuse seems to be limited to the abuse of cannabis, which is cultivated in several Pacific island countries. Cannabis is cultivated in Australia, Fiji and New Zealand and eradication campaigns are being conducted in all of those countries. In Samoa, Tonga and some other island countries, cannabis is cultivated mainly for personal use. Since the late 1980s, there has been a drastic increase in cannabis cultivation in Papua New Guinea, where the number of cannabis producers has been estimated at 30,000-40,000. The climate and the fertile soil of Papua New Guinea are conducive to the growing of a highly potent cannabis hybrid, significant quantities of which are consumed locally or, increasingly, are smuggled overseas, mainly into Australia. Cannabis is being smuggled into Australia not only from Papua New Guinea, but also from South-east Asia.

Increasing cannabis abuse has been reported in Australia, Fiji, New Zealand and Samoa, and especially in Papua New Guinea. In Papua New Guinea, some severe health problems have been attributed to the abuse of hybrid cannabis varieties with a high THC content.

In New Zealand, a sharp increase in the seizure of poppy plants was noted in the period 1992-1993. Morphine and heroin for local abuse continue to be manufactured in clandestine laboratories in New Zealand using pharmaceutical products containing codeine that have been obtained by robbing or breaking into pharmacies. Heroin is smuggled into Australia and New Zealand out of South-east Asia. Major heroin seizures have been reported in Australia, where the abuse of heroin is considered a serious problem. Cases involving the abuse of opioid analgesics (for example, morphine sulphate) have been reported in New Zealand.

The smuggling of cocaine out of the United States and countries in South America is on the increase.

The picture is rather dismal. Laws of the Federal/State and Local Governments, bilateral treaties and efforts at international level to enforce the laws can go a long way in combating the evil forces being let loose by drug trafficking. The experience in the past has been that often when one route was plugged, another emerged keeping the supply lines of illicit drugs alive. Often there have been loopholes in the laws and monitoring has been weak, but the worst part is that the law enforcing agencies are in many countries in league with the drug lords and mafias. The authority of law must prevail over the forces of evil designs of the drug cartels. Therein alone lies salvation for the human race.

4

Commonly Used Drugs
Their Use and Effects

Most drugs and their derivatives have acquired slang nomenclatures over the years. The addicts refer to them by names that are often different from 'dictionary words'. With a view to familiarise the reader with the slang names, they have been used simultaneously with the chemical or pharmaceutical nomenclature. This will be helpful to the readers as they read about these drugs in newspapers or magazines where the drugs are often referred to by the slang names.

In recent years, drugs have been used by athletes for improving their performances even though their use disqualifies the competitor from the event even after the medal has been awarded. Information about such steroids has also been provided since their use in high doses can pose a severe health problem.

The use of a specific drug, generally, depends upon its easy availability. The change in pattern of supply of a particular drug influences the demand for the particular drug as well as the demand for some substitute. Drugs contain chemicals that are used to alter the state of mind. 'They alter perceptions and behaviour by changing conscious awareness' – (Crooks and Steine – 1988). Most of the drugs induce physiological dependence on the drug abuser. The abuser feels a severe craving for the drug. Sometimes, to avoid withdrawal symptoms, abusers maintain a certain level of drug in their body as the withdrawal symptoms may be hard to bear. Other drugs that do not create physiological dependence lead the addict to psychological necessity. This necessity may be in terms of freeing the mind from frustrations or depressions. In these cases, one may find the drug 'pleasurable'. Tolerance to one drug may be overcome by the use of multiple drugs or gradual increase in the quantity of substance. One-time enjoyment can lead to disasters — the addict may suffer from several mental disorders or physiological diseases causing even untimely death.

Some commonly used drugs and their effects on one's total personality structure have been discussed in the following pages in order to create an awareness about the gravity of the drug syndrome.

Heroin

The medicinal term for heroin is 'Diamorphine'. It belongs to the opiate drug family. It is a white powder with a bitter taste. Illicit heroin may vary in colour from white to dark brown depending on the impurities left in it during production or the presence of additives such as food colouring coco or brown sugar.

The main active ingredient of opium is morphine. Heroin is a derivative of morphine. Heroin, used for medicinal purposes, works as a powerful pain-killer in the post-operative stage. It is also used for making pain in terminal stages of cancer bearable. It helps in bringing a distressing cough under control in serious lung conditions. Medicinal morphia is produced with great care and is dispensed with medical considerations.

Heroin is used by the addicts in multiple ways. It can be sniffed, swallowed, smoked or injected. When injected or inhaled in the form of fumes, it poisons the blood, damages the veins and infects the liver. Injecting heroin poses the additional risk of the addict contacting AIDS through the infected needle. Using common needles is a common practice among the addict groups. Prolonged use of heroin can be fatal.

Commonly used slangs for this drug are H, Boy, Brown sugar, Caballo, Chinese red, China, Crap, Doojee, Harry horse, Junk, Mexican mud powder, Scag, Smack, Stuff, Thing etc. Physical dependence may develop in weeks when taken by way of injections regularly. Psychological dependence can develop much earlier even when heroin is smoked.

Withdrawal symptoms begin eight to 24 hours after the last dose of the drug. The usual symptoms are aches and pains, misery of a chesty cold or a bout of diarrhoea which may last for about 24 hours. The weakness lasts for much longer periods. Severe symptoms of withdrawal include cramps, sleeplessness, vomiting,.alternating shivering and sweating etc. These symptoms may last for a week or even longer. Long-term effects of heroin are very severe as the addict may do anything to get the supply of the drug. Besides cheating or stealing, one can even beg to get the drug.

LSD

L.S.D. in its full form stands for Lysergic Acid Diethylemide. The acid occurs naturally in a fungus of rye.

The psychotomimetic effects of the acid were discovered accidently in 1943. A chemist took some L.S.D. and began experiencing the effects now known as a 'trip'. He noticed a sense of vertigo and restlessness. It was accompanied by bizarre visions and bright colours. A small amount of LSD may lead to distorted sensations. It is also known as mind-expanding drug.

Some of the common slangs used for L.S.D. are Acid, Beast, Big D, Blue Cheer, Blue Heaven, Brown Dots, Californian Sunshine, Chocolate Chips, Cup Cakes, Haze, Orange Mushrooms, Paper Acid, Royal Blue, The Hawk, Wedges or Window pane. L.S.D. is frequently sold in the form of tablets, thin squares of gelatin (window panes) or paper impregnated with the chemical ('blotter acid'). For a psychedelic trip, 100 to 250 micro grams are used. Paper tablets are often sold on the streets.

L.S.D. users describe their experiences as being out of the body and other hallucinations. Such hallucinations can be fatal as the users may jump from a height with a view to flying in the air. The 'trips', as the experiences are referred to, may not always be pleasant. There may be experiences comprising situations of being trapped dangerously. In the case of L.S.D. the psychological dependence is more acute than physical dependence. Subsequent doses of the drug are relatively less effective. 'Psychotic reaction' may develop after long term use of the drug.

Barbiturates

These belong to the group of drugs classified as hyno-sedatives used for inducing sleep among patients. The physician uses it to calm nervous conditions. In common parlance these are referred to as sleeping pills. Barbiturates can be extremely dangerous when taken in overdose or in combination with alcohol. They can cause coma and even death. Death occurs as a result of cardiovascular complications and respiratory arrest.

Long-term users of barbiturates face a much higher risk of contacting bronchitis and pneumonia. The addict develops skin rashes, irritability, depression and emotional instability. Cutting off supply can make the addicts turn violent and in extreme cases even unconscious. Withdrawal symptoms include anxiety, trembling, abdominal cramps, hallucinations, delirium, fits and even death. "A larger and larger dose to make him sleep, it does not take a larger and larger dose to kill him." ('Peter Parish').

The drugs are known by a number of slang words. They are Barb, Block Busters, Blue Birds, Blue Decils, Blue Dragons, Marshmallow, Reds, Mexican Reds, Nebbics Nimbies, Peanuts, Binks, Rainbows, Red and Blues, Red Birds–Red Devils, Sleeping Pills, Stumblers Yellow Jackets, Yellows or just Dolls.

Crack

It is an alkaloid in the leaves of erythroxylon coca, a hardy plant of the Anean Highlands of South America. The plant does not grow in India. The crop is legally cultivated for local consumption. But a part of it is illegally converted into coca paste and then smuggled to clandestine laboratories producing cocaine hydrochloride. The leaves are chewed by the natives of South America for refreshment and relief from fatigue. Cocaine as a local anaesthetic has been largely substituted by synthetic substances. Its medicinal applications are now restricted to ear and nose surgery. While the demand for licit cocaine has been going down, the supply of illicit cocaine has been rising.

Illicit cocaine is sold in the form of powder mixed with lactose. It is administered by sniffing or snorting and by intravenous injection. It is considered a status drug for 'recreational use'.

Cocaine causes increased heart beat rate and blood pressure. The other effects produced are rise in body temperature and increased metabolic rate. Regular sniffing can cause severe damage to the lining of the nose. The toxic effects of the drug include fainting, delirium, convulsions and respiratory failure. Patients who try to overcome its temptations accept that 'cocaine is greedy — the more you take, the more you need'. The only thing keeping a lid on its use is limited availability and high costs. The commonly used slangs for cocaine are Bernice, Big C, Coke, Dream, Flake, Girl, God Dust, Heaven Dust, Nose Candy, Paradise, Rock, Snow White etc.

Cannabis

It is the most widely used non-medical drug. It is also referred to as the Indian hemp. Cannabis sativa is widely distributed throughout the temperate and tropical regions of the world. The plant has been cultivated for centuries for the hemp fibres of the stem, the seeds of which are used in food mixtures and the oil as an ingredient of paint as well as for the biologically active substance contained in its leaves and flowering tops. The plant is grown extensively in Jamaica, Colombia, Mexico, Africa, India and the Middle East. The principal psycho-active substance in cannabis is thought to be delta-9-tetrahydrocannabinol (THC), a unique chemical found nowhere else in nature. In addition to delta-9-THC, cannabis contains other cannabinoids and chemicals. As a psycho-active drug, cannabis is smoked in the form of a loosely rolled cigarette. It can also be brewed in a drink or mixed with food.

Marijuana

Known as bhang or ganja in India Marijuana is prepared from cannabis plant by drying the leaves and flowerings of the plant to make a tobacco-like substance. It is known as recreational drug and is second in popularity after alcohol.

The commonly used slangs are Acapulco Gold, Broccoli, Bush, Dry High, Gage, Grass, Griffo, Hay, Hewys, Hard, J.Ray, Jane, Mary Jane, Mota, Mutah, Pahama Red Pod, Pot, Reafer, Sativa, Smoke, Stick, Tea, Weed, Dynamite, Ganja, Joint, Refear etc. Pot, Ganja and Joint are popular slangs for marijuana in India.

Hashish

Known by the name 'charas' in India, hashish is also a secretion of the cannabis plant. The drug soaked resinous secretions are dried and compressed into many sizes and shapes such as small balls, cakes or sheets. The slang terms used for hashish are Black Russian, Hash, Kif, Quarter Moon, Soles etc.

The reaction to this drug is increased talkativeness, hilarity, intoxication and a feeling of relaxation. The drug slows down concentration and mental functions impair muscular co-ordinations.

Heavy doses of cannabis substances can affect not only the heart and lungs but also the brain, liver, lymphatic glands including the body's immune system and the reproductive system. It can also cause cancer.

Withdrawal syndrome is characterised by insomnia, decreased appetite, and sudden loss of weight etc.

Amphetamines

The drug was widely prescribed for depression about two decades ago. Its non-medical use was confined to self- treatment by people to keep awake. Today, this group includes drugs such as dexedrine and ritalin. Both drugs are prescribed for the treatment of narcolepsy (sleeping sickness) and hyper-activity in children. Durophet is given to reduce appetite.

Amphetamine is also available as inhaler. Abuse of inhaler has become popular among students and prisoners.

The effect of a single dose lasts for about 3-4 hours leaving a feeling of tiredness. Amphetamines abuses also lead to suicide, homicide, assault and several other violent reactions. Other effects include blood clots, abscess of lungs, unclear speech, tremors etc. It can also result in amphetamine psychosis which is considered to be very similar to paranoid schizophrenia.

Withdrawal may cause cramping, nausea, convulsions and depression. Depression reaches its peak in 48 to 72 hours. It remains accute for a day or two. It is more dangerous to combine this drug with other drugs such as alcohol, heroin or barbiturates.

Commonly used slangs for amphetamines are Beans, Bennies, Black beauties, Black birds, Black mollies, Bumble bees, Cartwheels, Chalk, Chicken powder, Co-pilots, Crank, Crossroads, Crystal, Dexies, Double cross, Eye openers, Hearts, H Jelly beans, Lighting, Meth, Miniberries, Nuggets, Oranges, Pep pills, Speed, Roses, Thrusters Truck drivers, Turnabouts, Uppers, Ups, Wake-ups, etc. 'Speed' is the most commonly used slang in India for Amphetamines.

Opium

Opium is a mixture of about eighteen nitrogen containing agents known as alkaloids. It is derived from the poppy plant. India and Turkey have traditionally been the only two countries under world regulations which could produce opium legally. Turkey banned its production in 1974. In India, it continues to be grown in U.P., Rajasthan and Madhya Pradesh. Its medicinal value was that of a pain reliever. It was also used in the treatment of diarrhoea and dysentery. Morphine, the derivative used for relief from pain, is marketed in the form of white crystals, hypodermic tablets and preparations that could be injected. Addicts use it in more than one way such as intramuscularly or intravenously. Codeine is produced from morphine which produces analagesia, sedation and respiratory depression. Another ingredient of opium is tuebaine which produces stimulant rather than depressant effects. Heroin, which has been discussed earlier, is also an opium derivative.

Opiate addicts experience withdrawal symptoms within eight hours if they do not get their fresh dose. Initial symptoms are tearing eyes, running nose, perspiration, restlessness, and an intense desire for the drug. The symptoms reach their peak in about 40 hours. The addict individual becomes allergic to food and water coupled with vomitting, sweating which in turn leads to dehydration. It could further deteriorate into delirium or mania.

Tranquillizers or Depressants

Depressants, when taken under medical advice, can be beneficial in symptomatic treatment of insomnia, relief from anxiety, irritability and tension. Taken in excessive amounts, they produce intoxication like alcohol. In marked contrast to the effect of narcotics, intoxicating uses of depressants invariably result in impaired judgement, slurred speech and loss of motor co-ordination. They may also induce drowsiness, sleep stupor, coma and possible death. Tolerance to depressants develops rapidly, extending the intake capacity while narrowing the range between an intoxicating and a lethal dose. The person who is unaware of the dangers on increasing dependence will often seek prescription from several physicians concurrently increasing the daily intake upto 10 or 20 times the recommended amount. Members of the drug subculture often use 'depressants' as self medication to lull the 'jangled nerves' brought on by the use of stimulants, to quell anxiety of 'flashbacks' or to help them through 'withdrawal' from heroin. Depressants serve as a means of suicide common among women.

Symptoms of depressant abuse are coma, cold and clammy skin, weak and rapid pulse and low blood pressure. In its mildest form, the abstinence from depressants is characterized by anxiety, agitation, apprehension, loss of appetite, nausea, vomitting, palpitation, sweating, fainting, insomnia and muscular spasms.

Some of the commonly used tranquillizers are benzodiazepines, librium, valium and ativan etc. Tranquillizers are never to be taken with alcohol.

Mescaline or Peyote

It was used as an aid to relaxation and to enhance religious thoughts and also as a source for higher level of spiritual awareness. Dom is chemically related to mescaline and the amphetamines. Under the popular street name of STP (standing for Serenity, Tranquillity and Peace) the drug first won acceptance on the west coast of U.S.A. where it was popular for sometime. One of the most unpleasant effects of these drugs is nausea and vomitting lasting for two hours before the trip starts. Dilation of pupils, increase in heart beats and increased blood pressure are some other effects of the drug.

Mushrooms

These are other hallucinogenic substances which contain psilocypin and psilocin whose effects are similar to those of LSD. One of the users reported experience of colours and speed of movement with traffic moving frighteningly fast. The danger of accidents is very severe with all stimulating drugs.

Angel Dust

Its other names are PCP (phecyclidine), animal tranquillizer, Hog, Killer weed or Peace pill. Angel dust is the most popular street name. It is available in crystalline powder form.

It was first used as a street drug in San Francisco in 1967. During the last 15 years, it has become very popular in U.S.A. spreading among teenagers. It is considered to be one of the most dangerous among drugs. Low doses may produce paranoia and perceptual distortion while high doses may cause convulsions and catalepsy (abnormal sleep). In such cases, death can result from drowning, accidents etc.

Anabolic Steroids

Sportsmanship which once stood for playing the game in the spirit of the game is being increasingly substituted with 'win the game at any cost and by all means'. The use of steroids came into existence because of the change in the concept of competing in games and sports, specially where two or more nations are involved. Steroids are used to make the body strong and perform beyond its normal capacity. Sometimes even the user-competitor does not know about steroids being given to him by his coach, authorities or the doctors under the mask of vitamins.

The group of these drugs includes dianabol, stromba, durabolin etc. These drugs disturb hormones which may even cause infertility. In the long run, steroids have serious effects on blood. Cancer, coronary artery diseases and strokes are common dangers.

Caffeine/Nicotine

These are usually used as stimulants. Caffeine is found in tea, coffee, chocolates and other carbonate drinks. A little amount of caffeine gives boost to physical energy or mental alertness. It is like making the horse run faster by whipping. The energy does not come from the whip. High doses of caffeine can cause headache, insomnia, loss of appetite, irritability etc. People who take several cups of tea or coffee may suffer from these problems. Dusek and Girdano (1980) studied the effect of caffeine on children and found that children who take tea or caffeine suffer from anxiety disorders and learning difficulties. Caffeine consumption increases heart beat rate and blood pressure. People develop psychological dependence and when they are not served with the usual quantity, they feel restless and 'something missing'.

Nicotine is consumed by taking tobacco either in the raw form or through smoking. People who smoke claim that it has a stimulating effect. It develops physiological dependence. Withdrawal symptoms include craving, cramps in stomach, insomnia, anxiety, lack of concentration etc. Smoking is one of the accepted causes in the development of lung cancer.

Alcohol

Medical model recognises alcoholism as a progressive disease that can be divided into symptomatic phases. It differentiates between addict and non-addict drinkers. The addict drinker experiences a loss of control while the non-addict drinker does not suffer from such a feeling. The predisposition to loss of control is a chain reaction (Jellinel 1960). The reaction stems from psychological conflicts or social situations that initiate drinking eventually leading to physical demand for alcohol. In this process the body tissues acquire tolerance to alcohol and cell metabolism adapts to it.

On the other hand, the psychic model emphasises that alcohol is taken by an individual who is sensitive to tension of his psychic conflicts, has difficulty in dealing with them and seeks escape from the stresses of life rather than facing them. McCurdy's comments have great significance — 'The alcoholist is, before he touches a drop, an abnormal person'. Carver, in his article 'The Psychology of the Alcoholist' describes, 'The alcoholist is a highly sensitive, self indulgent individual with an extremely easily wounded *amour propre*.... Alcohol by producing euphoria, blunting the critical power and progressively relaxing inhibitions, permits of a flight from reality, which upto a certain point is pleasurable, but when it is pushed too far, regression proceeds to lower psychological developmental level, and the return of the repressed from these levels causes great anxiety and anti-social behaviour. Thus, in the long run, alcohol is liable to defeat the ends for which it is taken.'

Alcoholism, as in the case of some other drugs such as 'bhang', has its social dimensions too. In many societies and communities alcohol is very much a part of social rituals and customs. Drinking alcohol is, in such cases, accepted as a very natural and normal behaviour. Alcohol is now an integral part of European culture and many beliefs are prevalent with regard to the qualities of drinks or the advantages of alcohol consumption. The intergenerational transference of beliefs and practices take place in such cases.

The effects of the use of alcohol may be summarised thus : The immediate effects include hedonistic tendency, primitive behaviour, impairment of motor co-ordination, distorted speech and vision, confused thought process, increased sexual stimulation but lowered sex performance, blackouts, hangover-symptoms like fatigue, nausea and headache. Even 0.10 per cent alcohol in the blood substantially increases the chances of an alcoholic getting into an accident. The long-term effects are irreparable damage to liver cells, loss of appetite leading to several other disorders, risk of cancer, chronic fatigue, oversensitivity and depression. Use of alcohol hinders the absorption of vitamins leading to its deficiency and diseases caused by it. It can even lead to brain damage. It has been reported that more than 200,000 deaths occur every year due to causes associated with alcohol consumption. Alcohol is linked to two-thirds of all incidents of domestic violence and one-third of child abuse cases (Ziegler 1984).

Poets and authors have written so much eulogising 'wine'. Herd cites the rapid evolution of a cosmopolitan and permissive 'night club culture' in the first quarter of this century. Weikel Orland characterises urban Indian bars in America as 'Social Services Institutions'

Alcoholic beverages are often a part of religious rituals. They are offered to the deities to please them and bestow favours to the devotee. It is regarded as a magic substance near to God.

Alcohol and literature and fine arts have come to be associated in more than one country over the centuries. Many a British pub proudly display the names of the men of literature who frequented these places during their lifetime. It is even claimed that alcohol opened those vistas of imagination and creativity that otherwise might have remained dormant. Many artists nourish this notion. Musicians and performing artists hold similar views with honourable exceptions. All these notions have existed for so long that it is not easy to raise one's voice against the evils of alcoholism.

The Japanese have a proverb that aptly describes the relationship between alcohol and the addict, 'First the man takes a drink, then the drink takes a drink but ultimately the drink takes the man.'

Alcohol is the catalyst to violence including homicide and rape. Civilised societies have nearly given up their fight against alcohol and instead become dependent on excise revenues.

Glue Sniffing and Solvent Abuse

Solvent abuse involves every volatile substance used for domestic, cosmetic, or industrial purposes. They may be put in the following categories.

Table A
Summary of Drugs and their effects

Classification	Drugs	Usage	Medical Usage	Tolerance	Physiological Dependence	Psychological Dependence
Sedatives	Alcohol (ethanol)	Reduce tension Facilitate social interaction "Blot out"	No	Yes	Yes	Yes
	Barbiturates Nembutal (pentobarbital) Seconal (secobarbital) Veronal (barbital) Tuinal (secobarbital and amobarbital)	Reduce tension Induce relaxation and sleep	Yes	Yes	Yes	Yes
Stimulants	Amphetamines Benzedrine (amphetamine) Dexedrine (dextroamphetamine) Methedrine (methamphetamine)	Increase feelings of alertness and confidence Decrease feelings of fatigue Stay awake for long periods	Yes	Yes	No	Yes
	Cocaine (coca)	Decrease feelings of fatigue Increase endurance Stimulate sex drive	No	No (minimal)	No	Yes

Classification	Drugs	Usage	Medical Usage	Tolerance	Physiological Dependence	Psychological Dependence
Narcotics	Opium and its derivatives Opium Morphine Codeine Heroin	Alleviate physical pain Induce relaxation and pleasant reverie Alleviate anxiety and tension	Yes, except heroin	Yes	Yes	Yes
	Methadone (synthetic narcotic)	Treatment of heroin dependence	Yes	Yes	Yes	Yes
Psychedelics and Hallucinogens	Cannabis Marijuana Hashish Mescaline (peyote) Psilocybin (psychotogenic mushrooms) LSD (lysergic and diethyl-amide-25)	Induce changes in mood, thought, and behavior "Mind expansion"	No, except in research	No – possible reverse tolerance (marijuana)	No	Yes
Minor Tranquillizers	Librium (chlordiazepoxide hydrochloride) Miltown (meprobamate) Valium (diazepam) Others, *e.g.*, Compoz (scopolamine)	Alleviate tension and anxiety Induce relaxation and sleep	Yes	Yes	Yes	Yes

(*a*) *Adhesives*

The group includes cellulose paint, thinners, nail polish removers and other substances that contain toluene and acetone.

(*b*) *Dry cleaning material*

Trichloroethylene, trichloroethane and carbon tetrachloride are some of the commonly abused substances.

(*c*) *Aerosols*

These include hair sprays, deodorants, sprays, paints, household cleaners and polish sprays that contain fluorocarbons.

(*d*) *Fuels*

These solvents include lighter fuels and camping gas. The solvents are inhaled through plastic bags. The inhalation makes the person dizzy and confused and may even induce unconsciousness. Its long-term hazards are anaemia, leukaemia, brain damage, liver or renal damage etc.

The above description of commonly used drugs and the consequences of their abuse show how deceptive and fallacious are the commonly given justifications for use of drugs. For a very brief period, a person under the influence of a drug may find himself insulated against the hard realities of life. Once the effect is over the addict is again face to face with his problems, this time with diminished self-confidence, a new dimension being added to the problems. Drugs seriously threaten both the physical and psychological existence of the addict. As the psychological functions get distorted, his total personality suffers disintegration. Drug addicts suffer from malnutrition infections as most drugs induce loss of appetite. Syringes and needles used commonly by members of addict groups pose the additional danger of diseases like hepatitis or AIDS. The drugs commonly sold in the markets are frequently adulterated with cheaper mixtures necessitating either larger quantities for a kick or causing unforeseen damage to the body. The effect of drugs depends both on the drug and the individuality of the user. The quantity and the frequency of drug abuse also make a material difference. There may be slow poisoning of the mind and body or just instant death. Either way it is a human tragedy that is avoidable.

Summary of drugs and their effects may be seen in Table A (on pages 46 and 47)

How to Identify Drug Addicts ?

An early drug abuser may be no different from any other person unless observed by someone who is familiar with the signs that develop as one gets into drug abuse. The early signs are mostly ignored by parents who may be overconfident about their children. By the time everyone knows that the child is a drug abuser/addict, it is rather late to adopt preventive measures. The following are some of the distinguishing features of addicts that must be given due attention at a proper time.

(*a*) *Personality disintegration*

This is accompanied by abnormal behaviour such as lack of sequence in expressed thoughts, stammering, avoiding eye contacts while talking, frequently changing positions while standing, distortion in speech, emotional aggressiveness, sudden withdrawal, isolation, sudden changes in everyday behaviour such as getting easily excited or becoming violent, start crying or showing signs of emotional disbalance.

(*b*) *Change in value systems*

The drug abuser may show disregard for established family and social values, and start believing in 'free sex' and 'free life'. The addict may resort to stealing and telling lies to cover up.

(*c*) *Sudden change in company and friends*

Old friends who do not take drugs or abhor them become meaningless to the addict. He chooses new company His peer group excludes neighbours and classmates. He has new friends with whom he has one common activity *i.e.* of drugs.

(*d*) *Decline in school performances*

The drugs have a direct bearing on the addict performance at the school or college. His undesirable company, lack of concentration and allied side effects influence the academic performance. Any sudden drop in school performance accompanied by one or more signs should be the cause for a thorough investigation. The drug abuser loses interest in studies, starts abstaining from the class, does not complete home assignments and the quality of work decreases.

(*e*) *Physiological symptoms*

Drug abuse leads to loss in weight accompanied by itching on limbs, convulsions, cough and cold and scaly skin. Dark rings may come up around the eyes and there may be general expression of exhaustion all over.

(*f*) *Secretiveness*

The addict suffers from a feeling of guilt and chooses to be secretive about his movements and activities. There is a preference for being alone in one's room for longer durations keeping out normal company of the family members.

(*g*) *Irritability*

The addict gets irritated unusually. He is defensive and tries to explain when no such explanation is normally expected. He becomes irresponsible but hates to be told or reminded about his lapses.

(*h*) *Other changes*

The company of drug addicts enforces many other changes in behaviour. The addict's dress, hair styles, general facial appearance all undergo changes, often subtle and often loud.

Other areas that may get affected are choice of food, selection of literature and magazines, patterns of sleeping and use of electronic beepers as in USA. Late coming becomes frequent, may have frequent accidents. Forgetfulness increases.

Addicts also suffer from claustrophobia. They avoid crowded places and travelling in crowded buses/trains. Sometimes they get paranoid feelings that everybody around is creating troubles.

It is worth noting that a number of changes in behaviour, many of them congruent to those illustrated above also occur in the adolescent stage. One has to be careful in analysing behavioural changes. It would be risky to brand a child as an addict at the first sign of a behavioural change. What needs to be done is that behavioural changes should be intelligently monitored to be sure whether they are taking place in the natural sequence of growth or are coming up as a side effect of drugs to which the adolescent might be getting addicted.

5

Socio-economic Factors Influencing Drug Abuse

'I don't want to be back home, nobody cares.'

'I have so much stress at the work place.'

'I start from home to go to my office but I don't go.

I don't come back to my home either.'

> 'I want some thrill in life, my friend told me try this — you will fly like a bird high in the sky, you will swim like a fish in the sea...excitement all over.'

'I see no meaning in life. It is so boring.'

These are some of the commonly made statements by drug addicts. There could be numerous reasons for drug abuse. They may relate to environment, self, physiology, family, peer group etc. One or more of these reasons could drive a person to addiction to drugs including alcohol.

Some scholars believe that genetic influences play an important role in a person getting into the world of drugs. Others believe that it is not 'nature' but 'nurture' that makes the difference. Lettieri, Sayers and Pearson (1980) surveyed 43 modern theories of drug abuse and classified them in four categories.

A. Biological Theories

These theories have their base in bio-medical model of physical addiction. These theories explain drug addiction as sensory excitation and deprivation.

B. Personality Theories

Drug addictive behaviour has been explained in terms of personality disintegration in which the individual's personality characteristics become dysfunctional.

C. Interpersonal Theories

These theories emphasise individual's relationships with significant others. These recognise the parental and peer group influence and perceive drug abuse as maintaining one's identity in the family or community.

D. Socio-cultural Theories

These theories see the role of drugs in the larger social context of economic, racial and cultural differences in the society.

The causes that have emerged through interaction with addicts/abusers or through researches in that area are discussed here.

1. Establishing Oneself

In today's highly competitive world, there is an eternal struggle to establish oneself. This struggle becomes more severe in societies that do not have much to offer by way of economic security. In India, as in many more developing countries, the problem of unemployment among the youth has been causing great social unrest. The youth is under constant pressure and forced idleness. Neither the parents nor the society are sympathetic to the unemployed youth even though their unemployment is often the result of factors beyond their control. All these factors acting in combination result in deviant behaviours, one being drug abuse.

2. Symbol of Modernity

Drug abuse is perceived as a reaction to the so-called 'outmoded hypocratic lifestyles' of older generations. Due to the 'pub-culture' specially in the metropolitan cities, use of drugs has come to stay as a fashion or symbol of modernity. Old traditions make the youth feel 'odd man out' in their peer group. The boy or girl with a cigarette in one hand and a glass of hard drinks in the other is 'progressive' and 'courageous', otherwise one is branded as *bhaiya* or *behenji* of the elite group — both terms used in a derogatory sense. This culture is not limited to adult groups. Smoking, drinking beer and other drinks have become common even in school parties, birthday parties and other social celebrations where everybody participates in dancing alongwith drinks.

Modern societies, both in developed as well as developing countries, have varied divisions. It is not possible for those on the lower rung to imitate totally the lifestyles of those placed higher to them. But certain things can always be imitated to give the satisfaction that 'I too can do what the rich or the elite do'. Drugs or alcohol are one such thing. People from lower strata of society often take to drugs or alcohol as it is the 'in-thing' among the rich and elite social groups.

3. The Idle Time

A study conducted by S. Subramanium on student population in the city of Madras (1980) shows that generally the students have 600 to 1000 hours of free time per year. This time is in addition to the two months of summer vacation. Most students have no hobbies or leisure time activities that could keep them engaged during these periods. So they choose the easily accessible pubs or joints. Filling up the idle time, thus, emerges as a very relevant reason for drug or alcohol addiction.

4. The 'Do Me' Generation

More changes have taken place in human society during the last few decades than those that took place in the last few centuries. With these changes has come a very distinct change in the attitudes of the present generation. For centuries, it was believed in the Indian society that the young had a duty to maintain the old who spend the best part of their life trying to bring them up with utmost sacrifices. But now the society comprises a 'do-me' generation where expectations of younger generation are too high. The present-day generation expects that everyone around them must do things for them. Any failure is blamed on something that was not provided. This attitude creates two complications. The expectations of help from outside often leads to an atrophy of internal effort. Secondly, since no amount of external support can suffice, there is the lingering feeling that enough has not been done. This frustration becomes a temptation to 'escape' from real life struggles and blame everyone for non-achievement.

In this process one's own abilities and initiative take a back seat. Self-dependence is regarded as something fit only for the children of not-so-rich parents. Hard work and struggle have got replaced by 'do-me' conceptions. The smallest non-achievement leads the youth to the drug trap as they do not know how to face it.

The not-so-well-to-do boys and girls feel outcasted at their inability to compete with others and take to drugs as a measure of escape from the frustration and also to show that they are in no way inferior to their richer peers.

Surprisingly both the frustration of achievement among the very rich and the frustration of deprivation among the not-so-rich drive young boys and girls to drugs or alcohol.

5. **The Isolation**

The mad race for high achievements in career often leads to neglect of many other related areas of life. The high achiever may be socially aloof as he feels others are not upto his standards of achievement. He quietly forgets that brilliance in one area is no guarantee of success in another. The main belief that 'he is better than others' keeps him aloof from the rest. The high achiever, thus, becomes the victim of a self-imposed loneliness.

True, there is not enough room at the top. But it is not necessary to stay at the top for all times having reached there. Men who climbed the Everest did not stay there for all times. Having scaled the peak, they came down and found useful occupations other than reaching the top for the rest of their lives. The achiever has to share his prosperity with the rest if he wants to escape loneliness.

The loneliness syndrome is not exclusive to the high achiever. The non-achiever is often unwilling to try in other areas for which he may be better suited. People have fancy ideas about their capabilities and refuse to revise them even after successive failures. Non-achievement in such cases makes them believe that it is the end of the world so far as they are concerned.

The lonely high-achiever and the frustrated low-achiever are both vulnerable to drug abuse.

6. **Where Ignorance is not Bliss**

Drugs are now a trans-continental multi-billion dollar trade. The traffickers are perpetually searching for new markets and new customers. With a view to spread addiction, drugs are mixed in commonly used food items like chocolates. Drugs are sometimes passed off as vitamin tablets to school children. The users being ignorant of the contents find the new variety so different and unknowingly get hooked to drugs. Once the young people have got addicted, the traffickers extract high prices.

7. **Faulty Family Patterns**

Quite often addiction among young boys and girls is caused inadvertently by the parents who may be very keen to see that their wards suffer from no social inferiority. Families where the parents have suffered serious economic deprivations in their early careers have a tendency to insulate their children from all that they suffered during their own childhood. There is undue and often excessive pampering. Children of such parents often have access to pocket money disproportionate to their capacity to discriminate between what is a good buy or what is bad in the long run. In the school or college, such children are easily identified and become a prey to those who are already addicts.

The rich parents often provide expensive games and modes of recreation to their children as a substitute for their care and time. Such children have access to lots of pocket money. They just don't know what to do with their unsupervised time and money. Drugs, once introduced to such children, take quick roots. By the time the parents note the changes in their children's behaviour, it may be too late.

In poor families, too, lack of time for attending to children and meeting their emotional needs lead to irresponsible behaviour on the part of the children. A drug peddler in the neighbourhood is a far greater possibility in their case. Children may be lured into the trade with the temptation of easy and quick money. The peddler may thereafter introduce them to drugs. Once they have fallen into the trap, they need not even be paid for doing his job.

A major check to children getting into the drug trap lies in good parent-child relationship. Where parents take interest in what their children like to do, the chances of their going astray are few. Even if deviation does occur it soon gets detected. De-addiction is much easier in cases where parental support is available to the younger people in the family.

Often parents find the normal activities of a child or younger members of the family too childish for them. 'I can't go about flying kites at this age' may be a common expression of unwillingness to join with the younger members of the family in what is satisfying to them.

It is obvious that two generations cannot have the same interests. The father may get pleasure from books. The son may like to have a game of badminton or just a day out. What is desirable is that there be a balance between what members of the family do singly and what they do jointly. The greater the time that the family spends in joint activities the lesser the chances of younger people being tempted into undesirable modes of seeking excitement.

It is also important that parents do not cause unusual stress to their young ones. Parental expectations these days are very high. So often a parent expects his child to be what the elder could not be in his lifetime. In this expectation, the child's aptitude and basic and inherent capabilities have no place. A mother wanted to be a doctor. She could not. So the daughter must be a doctor. The fact that the daughter wants to be a painter or a dancer would just not be acceptable keeping the daughter under perpetual distress. In such circumstances children become deviant at the first opportunity. Anybody or anything that offers them relief from this stress is welcome. Drugs often offer the easily available escape.

Often the teacher or a neighbour throws a hint that the boy or girl is showing symptoms of an unusual behaviour. The first instinct of the parents then is to defend their child and curse the informant making the matters worse.

Children of the families that lack proper communication system which builds up trust and confidence easily fall into the drug net. If the family has occasions where each member of the family gets time to talk, share and care, children would feel more secure and confide to their parents if any unusual overtures were made to them. Under-protection where children get no directions can be as serious a cause for getting them into drug habits as over-protection where parents are too 'authoritative' or 'possessive'.

The most damaging reason for children getting into the drug net is often 'broken homes'. Divorced parents living singly or children living with a stepfather or a stepmother are most prone to emotional hangups which hinder the normal personality growth. Children brought up in such situations are relatively more prone to drug temptations. R.H. Blum *et al* (1970) stated "conflict in the family leads to common problems between parents and child, increasing the child's vulnerability to drug abuse".

8. Families Involved in Anti-social Activities

Couriering and peddling of drugs or illicit liquor is almost an occupation with certain groups of people. They may or may not have cover occupations. Drug pushers resort to sales along with some regular professions like running a corner store or just know their clients and make supplies on demand. Sooner or later other members of the family, wife or children also join. Social censure that accompanies drugs no longer operates once a child or family member knows that one of them is involved in drug business. Other petty criminals take to drug peddling as a side vocation. In such cases also, other members of the family, not indirectly involved in the drug business, are tempted to use drugs as and when available. The son may just pinch some from the father's stock of trade. Over a period he or she may get addicted and may follow in the footsteps of his seniors.

9. Parental Models

Alcohol is a symbol of sophistication in many social groups. Business contracts are finalised over rounds of drinks. Such parties may be held in clubs or even at home in case of highly placed people. The father and mother, both, may take hard drinks to entertain their guests. Children may not partake of such parties but they get the impression that there is nothing unsocial about drinks. Once this inhibition is removed, it becomes very difficult to explain to children that drinks are alright for 'papa' but not for others in the house. D.B. Kandel in a study of 1978 showed that if there is a high family substance abuse, even of nicotine or alcohol, such behaviours are more likely to become internalised.

The same may be true about conventionally used drugs. Children would rather not wait till they grow into adults. They would like to have a kick at the first opportunity.

10. Genetic or Biological Reasons

The role of genetics in vulnerability to drugs cannot be denied. The evidence of hereditary tendencies that determine addiction is revealed in a study by Mclearn of the Institute of Behavioural Genetics, University of Colorado. This study on rats and mice provides evidence that alcohol and differential sensitivity to its effects have hereditable basis.

Other studies show that alcoholism tends to run in families. In a study of 259 hospitalised alcoholics made by Winokur *et al* (1970) it was revealed that slightly over 40 per cent had a parent usually the father who was an alcoholic. Goodwin *et al* (1973) and Goodwin and his colleagues (1974) concluded in their studies that it was being born to an alcoholic biologic parent rather than being raised by one that increased the risk of the son becoming an alcoholic.

11. **Peer Group Influence**

The peer group is very determining influence in drug abuse studies. Where all others take alcohol or drugs, even a person who is otherwise not interested may feel tempted to indulge. As per Social Learning Theory, drug use is conceived of in terms of social factors interacting with the individual factors within the social context. Here drug abuse is a learned behaviour and peer group is one best source of acquiring certain types of behaviour patterns. Peer group culture may be a culture of 'do-drugs' culture. They display 'What's the big deal ? Everybody does it.' This (everybody does it) concept is more popular in highly developed countries like America or Europe.

12. **Influence of Movies and the Media**

The movies today glamourise drinking. The hero resorts to drinks when he is depressed. The villain celebrates through drinks. The wamp drinks and everybody else who matters drinks. So what children may not see in the family, they see on the screen — big or small.

T.V. has affected family life in one more way. It has reduced the time available for intercommunication among the family members. It has the snowballing effect of creating misunderstandings that do not resolve of unfulfilled expectations that are not talked about and of poor academic performance due to inattentiveness on the part of the children. No wonder they call it the idiot box. It seems to have made an idiot of otherwise educated families.

The contributing factors seem to be spread over a very large expanse. Many of them are direct fall-out of the modernisation process with its emphasis on consumerism. Any precept that in effect amounts to slowing down the pace of unbridled consumerism is unlikely to find favour with masses in the developing and the least developed countries. They would rather like to reach western heights and then think of its adverse reactions.

The initiative, however, has to come from somewhere. Each group has to find its own initiators. Those highly placed on the economic ladder would need rethinking on the cracking family support systems. Those economically deprived will need to think in terms of positive economic achievements without overthrowing established social norms. The challenge is gigantic. But so is human ingenuity to cope with problems.

6

Psychological Correlates of Drug Abuse

"Drug abuse is a regressive symptom and the basic issue is the treatment of the underlying conflicts. It has meaning in relationship to the intrapsychic state of the patient..."

The definition states that in order to deal with the problem of drug abuse it is important to know the intrapsychic state of the person.

Psychological disorders in general are explained through personality characteristics. Addictive behaviour is one which is manifested in personality structures as drug dependence is in itself a serious psychological disorder. On the other hand, Woody and Blaine 1979; Dorus and Senay 1980; Rounsaville *et al* 1982 opined that drug dependence frequently occurs with other psychiatric disorders such as depression. People who are drug addicts generally suffer from anti-social feelings, phobias, psycho-sexual dysfunctions etc.

Introvertive vs Extrovertive Personalities

Eysenck theory of personality (1957a) defines extrovertive personalities as having strong inhibitions and weak excitation while in the case of introvertive personalities, the tendency is opposite. This theory can be correlated with the drug dependence behaviours. Cockett and Marks in 1969 in a study stated that users of stimulant drugs were more introvertive, shy and retiring than non-users and those who were using depressant drugs were seen to be more extrovert than non-users (Smart, 1965). Hogan *et al* (1970) opined that drug users are more socially poised, open to experience, adventurous, impulsive and pleasure seeking.

Wilson and Kennard in 1978 noticed that initial introversion experienced in abusers might be the result of drug abuse itself as he saw a fast change in the patients from introversion to extroversion.

Similarly Knight and Prout (1955) have found drug addict patients to be shy, self-conscious, insecure and reserved. all factors relating to introversion. These researches show that personality type is significantly associated with drug abusive behaviours though researches are contradictory in providing any specific directions.

Depression

A strong positive correlation has been found in several researches between depression and use of drugs and alcohol. Persons under depression use drugs as a defence mechanism process. Paton and Kandel 1978 found that two factors depressiveness and normlessness are responsible for drug abuse. Drug users in general have a feeling of inadequacy and depression (Angst 1971). Kielhotz and Ladewig in 1970 studied 120 juvenile drug abusers and found that they showed depressive reactions.

Coleman writes that a depressed person may turn to the excessive use of alcohol, or the excessive use of alcohol may lead to depression. Thus, depression, on the one hand, is a cause of drug abuse. On the other hand, it is a result of the drug abuse. Robbins study (1974) on the heroin addicts shows that many of the users experience strong depressed feelings.

Studies on cocaine use reveal that a quarter or more of users in early '80s had pre-existing depression and users thought that cocaine was anti-depressant or was helping mood disorders. (Gawin, F.M. and Kleber, H.D., 1986.)

The author, during the interviews with alcoholics and those using drugs like tranquillizers found that depression is one of the important causes among drug abusers which in turn is caused by 'frustration of non-achievements' in today's world of high competition. Next to depression are helplessness and aimlessness. Once out of the effect of drug, one is dragged into greater depressions. The chain goes on gradually diminishing the motivation to strive, compete and achieve. In the asphyxiated mental environment alcohol/drugs seem the only ray of hope.

Role Expectancies

Male and female role orientations differ to a great extent. Men are expected to be strong, masculine and 'he man' while females are expected to be identified with the traditional female role that is feminine, soft and dependant. When males and females are not able to identify their expected roles, a feeling of frustration and inferiority develops. Sometimes stress also develops when either a male or a female wants to cross the demarcation line of male and female roles. These feelings of stress, inferiority and tension lead people to consume liquor and drugs. Pratt (1972) and McClelland *et al*, 1972 stated that most of the young persons indulge in drug abuse behaviours to prove their masculinity, adequacy and competency. Wilsnack (1973a, 1973b) stated that females "manage to cope with their fragile sense of feminine adequacy for a number of years but when some new threat severely exacerbates her self doubts, she turns to alcohol in an attempt to gain artificial feelings of womanliness."

Sex Inhibitions

In most societies where sex is a taboo, use of alcohol or drugs is viewed as a catalyst to overcome inhibitions. In others, that is, free-sex societies, it is believed to boost sex functions.

The psycho-analysts also view alcoholism in males as expression of repressed sexuality and homo-sexuality. They contend that drinking works as an inhibition remover and helps in bringing up repressed urges. This theory has not got much support in researches as in the western societies male and females take drinks together and homo-sexuality is an accepted phenomenon. The question of repressed sexuality does not arise in such cases. However, use of alcohol and drugs for encouraging sex activity is a common response. There is a strong misbelief that alcohol or drugs improve sex-related functions and behaviours. In contrastive analysis of a sample of 200 drug addicts, it was found that 70 per cent alcoholics in America used drugs to boost sex functions. In India it was both for overcoming sex inhibitions and improving sex performance.

Anxiety

Individuals who are anxiety-prone suffer from the feeling of emotionality and inadequacy. They are over-responsive and impatient. These individuals develop lots of inferiority complexes and to achieve success, they resort to drug use. In order to cope with becoming an 'independent adult' they try to get immediate gratification of pleasurable impulses. The feelings of 'disintegrated personality' in which one is not able to take up adult roles becomes concerned with achieving a hedonistically structured environment for himself by using drugs. This leads to accepting oneself as an object of 'self-pity' and dependence. Gerald and Kornotsky (1954) found 50 per cent of the addicts suffer from either character disorders or inadequate personalities. The addicts were also found to be hyper-sensitive, self-conscious, less confident, pessimistic, insecure by Gilbert & Lombardi (1967). Case histories analysed by the author support the findings. Several researches have shown that drug users are reported to have worries, anxieties and disagreeable emotional feelings. They also exhibit neurotic and schizoid tendencies. (Hartgen 1959; Wilker 1963; Gilbert and Lombardi 1969; Smart and Jones 1970). Black and Heald's MMPI profiles of 1975 show some interesting results. The study states that drug abusers have a greater incidence of emotional dysfunction than alcoholics. Shanmugam (1979) finds that drug users scored high in neuroticism. King and Henry (1974) found dominance, radicalism, self-indulgence and aggression as higher and social inhibition and conscious development as lower among drug users than among others.

Rauchfleish (1971) states that addicts suffer from a conflict between 'id' and 'super ego'. It is an unbalanced fluctuation between controlled satisfaction of the 'id' impulses and one-sided submission to the denying demands of the super-ego.

During counselling sessions held by the author, several interesting aspects emerged to support the above results. Children of over-protective parents suppress their feelings of what they wanted to do. This was more true in Indian situations where children are not expected to discuss sex or related questions freely. With their suppressed feelings, they indulge in drug/alcohol... using behaviours to enjoy their 'id' feelings. When the effect of drug is over, they suffer from a feeling of guilt due to pressures of 'super ego'. This again pushes them to take drugs or alcohol. A vicious circle is formed. Gradually the strength of super-ego weakens.

Self-concept

To Hurlock (1972) the personality pattern can be thought of as a wheel where the spokes are the different personality traits and the hub is the concept of self. Self-concept is the determining factor of the thought processes of an individual and also forms the behaviour patterns. 'Self' may be defined in layman's terminology as 'some unique personality singled out from the rest of the world'. In technical terms it has been defined in a number of ways such as 'individual's private world of experiences', or a sense of self-worth or how others perceive the individual. Self-concept may also be defined in terms of 'what a person actually is' *i.e.* the 'real-self' and how he wants to be *i.e.* the 'ideal-self'. The degree of discrepancy in this 'real' and 'ideal' self leads to personality dysfunctions one of which is the 'addictive' behaviour. The higher discrepancy may be responsible to make a person feel that 'he has no worth in the society' when his ideals are too high. He may think 'he cannot achieve' them. The alcoholic or addictive behaviour results as a defensive attitude.

Curran and Patridge 1959 conclude that the awareness gap between 'real' and 'ideal' self leads to individuals to take drugs to overcome their fluctuations. Considerable deficiency in self-esteem among drug dependent patients has been reported by Gossop (1976), Carmichael *et al* (1977) and Jeroma *et al* (1978), Nyswander (1956) found drug addicts as exhibiting self-destructive tendencies and could be termed as 'Mesochist'. Drug addicts having greater disparity in self-image has been shown by Brehm and Back (1968). Most of the researchers interested in studying self-concept in relation to problem-behaviour have taken samples on alcoholics. The problem of drinking has been associated with low self-evaluations (Williams 1965; Corroll and Fuller 1969; Gross and Alder 1970). Alcoholics in general have been found to have a behaviour that show dissatisfaction with the characteristics of their body-image and a low level of self-esteem (Parades *et al* 1969).

Altering the State of Mind

Ronald Seigal, a psycho-pharmacologist, argued that there is an inherent need in human beings to alter their psyche or state of consciousness. No one gets perpetual thrill out of real life situations all the time. Those who are in search of thrills take to shortcuts by taking drugs for illusionary revelations. The motivational approaches to drugs suggest that men seek ecstasy stimulation, joy, approval of God by altering their state of mind by use of drugs and alcohol. The dreamy and ecstatic state which drugs produce make people feel they were in heaven beyond earth. Shaman, for example, uses various drugs for producing a condition of excitement in which he sees visions, makes prophecies, or drives out evil spirits. Charas has been a commonly used drug in some groups of sadhus as a shortcut to heavenly visions.

Zuckerman *et al* found that adolescents seeking high scores on tests for Sensation Seeking Scale also are likely to be users of nicotine, alcohol, drugs and to be sexually active. To get high kicks, thrills and sensations, use of drugs is being perceived specially by youths as essential.

In Search of Identity

An adolescent is 'half-child', 'half-adult', according to Ausubel (1954). It can be termed as an age of utter confusion and conflicts as the person does not know to which group he belongs. He develops his own value system most of the time incongruent with the prevailing norms. He does not want to act as a child any more but does not get accepted in the adult roles when he tries to express his views in decision-taking behaviours. Use of alcohol/drugs often comes as a form of aggression against self or as an expression of rejecting the prevailing social norms of 'so-called adults'. The drug abuse behaviour is also a reflection of assuming the adult roles earliest in search for an identity of his own which may be a mistaken or psuedo identity.

Perception of Drugs

In ancient culture, the use of drugs by the common man used to be perceived as 'unethical'. In modern societies total perception towards drugs and alcohol has changed. While the grown-ups consider it a necessity of life, the youth perceives it as the 'glamour of the life' Disco and fun of life are incomplete without a peg of whisky. A pro-drug attitude is taking its roots in India and other developing countries due to interactions with most modern societies of the world. It seems that drugs are an essential corollary of development: Interviews with the drug-abusers show that attitudes like 'death is inevitable; so why worry', 'there is only one life, why not have fun', or 'oh ! it wouldn't make me addict if I take drugs occasionally to get a thrill' are emerging. These attitudes are linked up with the desire of shirking from responsibilities and hard work. These favourable attitudes toward use of drugs are in a way projections of inner tendency for continued dependence on parents and withdrawal from facing the challenges of life.

The Curiosity

Human mind is inquisitive, rarely satisfied with what is known. It is in constant search of 'what happens when...? The quest, on the one hand, had been the fountainhead of several inventions, on the other hand, it worked as a source of deviant behaviours. Curiosity is much more intense when one is not allowed to act in a certain manner.The same is true in case of use of alcohol. 'My father drinks, my mother smokes, why am I denied to have a puff', says a curious child whose 'why' remains unanswered. At the first opportunity he tries to satisfy this 'why'. In today's world when drugs are characterised as 'mind expanding' or 'tools for concentration' or thrilling, the curiosity on the part of the newcomer seems to be natural.

Attention Getting Behaviour

Drugs have in a number of cases been found to be the substitute for excessive attention given to some children during their early childhood days. When this excessive attention is withdrawn for some reason, the children feel insecure. They take to drugs to get over their feeling of insecurity. Seeking parental care and concern acts as a factor responsible for drug abuse in some other cases also. These include children who have suffered parental neglect for reason of poverty or unduly large family size. Unsocial or errant behaviour on their part is a mechanism to seek attention. In highly developed societies, where single parenting, step parenting, foster parenting, child abuse and parental rejection are a growing phenomenon, children suffer from the trauma that often drives them into drug abuse.

Aldous Huxley (1954) stated "that humanity at large will ever be able to dispense with artificial paradises seems very unlikely. Most men and women lead lives at worst so painful, at the best so monotonous, poor and limited that the urge to escape, the longing to transcend themselves if only for a few moments, is and has always been one of principal appetites of the soul".

The narration seems to be self-defeating. Is human race so weak ? Is there no other way out ? There certainly are. Human ingenuity has only to apply itself to the problem as seriously as it did in moving out from the caves.

7

Prevention of Drug Abuse

Dr. Nils Bejerot (1983) viewed the problem of drugs like spread of malaria. He postulated that "malaria cannot be eradicated by hunting individual mosquitoes *i.e.* just the suppliers, drug problem cannot be treated just by 'treatment' alone. The requirement is a 'drainage of drug marshes". For that purpose a healthy environment must be created where the problem occurs. The immunity of the individual has to be strengthened in addition to reduction in drug supply. If that happens, the demand will be automatically reduced. Hence, to create a drug-free environment, prevention programme from macro to micro level is necessary.

A prevention programme aims at keeping the people away from ever touching the drugs, and keeping the users away from habituation. These programmes involve modification of the surroundings and environment and also a change in the feelings and attitudes of individuals with regard to drug use.

In order to make drug prevention programmes effective, it is essential to identify risk groups in the first instance. Similarly the risk factors need to be identified. Once that has been done, multi-model approaches to target the various systems responsible for drug accessibility and abuse are to be evolved. The prevention programmes may have to involve the individual, the families, schools, workplaces and community. Multiple approaches to solve the problem would include counselling, therapies, distribution of information, change in social values etc. The prevention programme has to be a continuous process to be effective. Only a continuous prevention programme can develop a healthy mind in the individual and a healthy environment in which the individual lives.

Public Health Model of Prevention

J.F. Jekel developed a model titled 'Public Health Approaches to the Cocaine Problem' (1987). The model could be applied to other areas of drug abuse too with modifications where necessary. Public Health is viewed as a triad composed of Host, Agent and Environment. A fourth equally important component is the Vector.

The Host : This relates to the potential drug user. Between the ages 15-40, most people must be considered as potential drug users. This age span is most prone to anxiety and stress. Many ups and downs confront the individuals during this period. One has to keep himself mentally as well as physically healthy to be able to cope up with these stresses. Resistance has to be built up to face situations that may not always be to one's liking. In the absence of the capacity to take shocks, one is likely to be pushed into drugs.

The Agent : The drug is the agent against whom prevention strategies have to be modelled as there is a continuous push and pull to use more and more drugs.

The Environment : This plays a very determining role. It is the easy availability of drug that needs to be checked to make a programme of public health effective.

The Vector : It is the drug distribution network. It includes the large mafias down to the local pusher.

Levels of Prevention

Primary Prevention

It involves measures to check the growth of the disease-forming process. Thus, there have to be programmes for promotion of general health as well as for providing specific protection against drug abuse.

Secondary Prevention

This involves early detection of the problem. The cases detected have to be provided the necessary treatment. Secondary prevention relates to only such cases that have not yet become hard addicts. Drug users who do not have serious problems and have not come to the stage of being 'dysfunctional' are covered in this category.

Tertiary Prevention

These programmes are aimed at preventing the negative effects of drug abuse through treatment (Tx.) and rehabilitation of addicts in whose cases the problems have been identified. Tertiary programmes include creating a body of informed and enlightened citizens and opinion leaders in the society. This is possible where the educational system incorporates within itself awareness to harmful effects of drugs. The awareness needs to be developed from early childhood in a manner that it does not provoke contra-suggestion.

In the light of the Public Health Model it is necessary that preventive measures are taken at community, school, workplace and family levels.

Prevention at Community Level

The concept of mental health has not gained popularity in developing societies the way it has been accepted in developed societies. Drug abuse is a multi-headed problem which can be combated only if more than one wing of the community joins together to fight. Community level efforts are also necessary because no individual or unit of the society can muster up enough resources to fight the various dimensions of the drug menace.

Individuals are trapped through a number of loopholes in the social systems. These loopholes have to be identified and plugged with joint effort.

The community's first effort has to be to identify the risk groups. These may be the poor youth living in areas that are cut off from the mainstream. They could also be the unemployed youth or the idle rich. Such identification ensures that the community's efforts and resources are not spread too thinly or wasted.

Then there are risk localities. Areas that are more prone include slums, lonely spots, or even the schools and colleges where westernisation in the name of modernisation is replacing the Indian value system.

Apart from risk groups and risk areas, the community has to tackle the problems that though strictly not within the ambit of mental health seriously affect it. These may work as a barrier in making any prevention programmes successful. These are social and economic problems for which the community may even need support from other agencies like the local bodies and the State and other voluntary organisations. For example, illiteracy may in many cases hinder the success of the prevention programmes. In such cases film shows, street plays and similar communication channels would need to be explored. Only the community can take up such measures. It is easier for the community to identify which drug is more easily accessible, and, therefore, popular. For example, opium may be the easily accessible drug in Rajasthan while cannabis may be more popular in the foot hills. After identification of risk groups, risk factors, hindrances in the prevention programme, source of the supply of drugs etc, effective prevention programme may be chalked out pooling all the resources available in the community. The prevention programme must follow the 'Development Programme' as per needs of the community. The following programmes may be organised at the community level:

Structured media campaigns may be launched by the community. Local magazines and newspapers are read with interest as they give news about matters with which the ordinary people find it easier to identify. These can be usefully exploited to carry and convey the social messages. The starting point could be an item serialising how an addict got out of the drug net and how he feels about it now. If the characters are known to the people, the message becomes very effective. When Mickey or Donald gives the message that 'drugs are harmful', it becomes more meaningful to their fans. Similarly, a 'he man' saying that he is a 'he man' as he has kept himself away from drugs all the time will be a very meaningful message to those who adore him as a hero. Teenagers, the most vulnerable group, can be best approached through such campaigns using advertisement strategies that commercial firms adopt to promote their products.

Five-star hotel conferences may not always be very helpful for results at the grassroot level. The message must come through and in a manner which the common people understand. There are folk performances in small towns that are usually very popular among the masses in India. Such gatherings and performances are occasions most suited for conveying the messages of keeping away from drugs. In Uttar Pradesh, there may be 'nautanki', in Maharashtra it would be a 'tamasha' and in West Bengal it could be 'jyatra'. These performances attract huge crowds. Street plays and puppet programmes can also be effectively used to bring out the desired results, specially in those areas where concentration of illiterate population is higher. An illiterate person cannot read a magazine or newspaper but such shows may knock every door of the house in the community.

Phone-in programmes can be very effective in cities with broadcasting facilities. Often the addict is shy or reluctant to disclose his identity. He doesn't even want to be seen going to a counsellor or a drug de-addiction clinic. He can use a phone-in programme from a public call booth and get the much-needed advice without being spotted as a drug addict. For successful implementation of such programmes, two or three persons may be put at the receiving end of the phone calls. They should be experts with adequate knowledge of drugs, their effects and information about drug de-addiction centres.

In addition the community may organise anti-drug poster contests, essay competitions, spot painting competitions and cultural programmes for conveying the message relating to drug prevention and de-addiction programmes. Awareness can also be created through pamphlets or advertisements through commonly used items such as reverse of bus tickets, match box labels, postal stamps and electricity or water bills proformas.

All these help in creating 'life skills' known as anti-drug value system in the society. In USA door-to-door campaigns were organised. These campaigns carried the message such as 'be smart, stay smart, don't start'. The U.S. Department of Education sponsored a 'Slam the Door on Drugs' campaign which ties with its 'School without Drugs Programme'.

Prevention programmes can be successful only if they are backed with developmental activities. The community must provide positive avenues such as recreational programmes, educational activities preferably involving talented members from the community. If there are enough worthwhile occupations available in the leisure time, people will be less tempted to resort to drug-related behaviour.

Summer vacations in schools are the time when many youngsters have all the time at their disposal. Unoccupied minds are most tempted to seek thrills in the drugs. This is the time when the community must provide activities such as hobby clubs, hikings, adventure tourism, health clubs, gyms. and similar programmes that would keep the faculties of mind and body engaged.

Organisation of such programmes is possible only if people from that community come forward and take the initiative. If the persons of a specific locality are involved, the whole community will be ready to own the programme. Hence a 'community base' is essential for prevention of drug abuse as 'outsiders' may be treated as 'unwanted' interferring in the personal affairs of the community. Resident artists, retired teachers, talented house-wives and other local talent should be harnessed to provide a forum where the creative abilities of the youngers find expression. Basic trust building is possible only if community people participate in the programme. Help may be taken from natural helpers *i.e.* those who are already working in the field. Teenagers must be involved in the Drug Prevention Programmes as their enthusiasm and idealism will develop confidence in people who are prone to drugs or are tempted to drug use.

Prevention Programmes at the Workplace

Drug abuse, irrespective of whether the drugs are hard ones or of the gateway category, affects the total work culture of the organization. The addicts drift into absenteeism, often for reasons physical and often for reasons emotional or even financial. The efficiency of the organisation depends on the contribution made by each one of the individual worker. When a group comprising the addicts is absent, the whole schedule goes out of gear. While the addicts suffer due to their misdeeds, all others suffer just because they are part of the organisation.

Drug abuse problems at the workplace are more severe and complex in developed societies. In countries like India, the incidence is restricted to smoking and use of alcohol. Cases of hard drug addicts have been reported from the freelancing artisans and independently functioning self-employed.

The problem of alcoholism among office workers arises from certain basic deficiencies in the organisational set-up, specially in public sector organisations where job security is relatively higher. Government offices in India and most developing countries are characterised by weak administration, over-staffing leading to insufficient work for the day and lack of answerability for performance. Assured of job security, the employees have enough time to idle away and the 'devil' takes his toll from among the empty minds. There are hardly any opportunities for higher achievement that would keep the workers motivated for higher organisational performance rather than idle addiction. The tendency among those who know the addict is either to 'hell with him' or to exploit him in his weak moments. Either way cases are not referred for any treatment or to de-addiction centres. The problem remains untouched.

Prevention programmes at workplaces have to start with stricter enforcement of disciplinary rules. In the private sector, where rules are strictly enforced, no employee can dare to have drinks during office hours or come to office in an intoxicated state. However, it is not uncommon in government offices for people to 'open the bottle' after office hours or even during the working hours. The position is specially bad in offices with public dealings where easy money is the rule rather than the exception.

The rules must be clearly known and enforced impartially. If there are detected cases, these must be isolated and be put under assistance programmes. They may need counselling, referral treatment or even rehabilitation depending on the nature and extent of addiction. Any organisation where there is enough motivation for better performance and also enough work for each employee is least likely to have in it the drug addicts. Of course, the social and family factors that operate outside the workplace will have their own influence. Drug addiction can be infectious if there are already a few and the fresh entrants have not been trained by way of induction/orientation programme to perform their assigned functions. The freshers would invariably have to go to the seniors for guidance frequently. The boss at the top may be inaccessible or be just concerned with performance. If the fresher gets frequent rebuffs for his low or non-performance, he is most likely to seek the company of those who may show him maximum sympathy although for ulterior motives. This is how the tribe of addicts increases in 'soft' disciplined organisations.

Freshers joining the Defence services are familiarised with techniques commonly used by spies of the enemy to rope in the freshers. Likewise, in case it is known that there is an addict group operating within the organisation, it should be part of the induction programme to warn the fresher against getting into the company of those people who may otherwise appear to be most receptive and helpful.

The supervisors have a special role to play in the organisations, in implementing programmes against drug abuse. It is they who can identify the addicts. Once identified, the addict would have to be counselled or referred to the specialist for such treatment as may be necessary. Some organisations just fire the person found to be indulging in drug use. That may solve the organisation's problem but create many more for the society at large. That is hardly any solution for if the society has addicts within, each organisation will get its share.

In industrial areas and places where workers reside in large numbers, there is need for counselling and de-addiction centres as much as the need for a primary health centre. In situations where there are financial limitations, the counseller may be attached to the health centre and operate from the same premises. He or she must, however, have the necessary professional background. It would not be worth-while if one of the functionaries is also assigned the job in addition to his or her own duties.

There have been cases where drug de-addiction centres are being run by the local police department. The advantage with such an arrangement is that addict-criminal nexus is best known to the police. So the department can easily identify the cases that need counselling or treatment. The disadvantage is that there is a stigma attached to going to something that is within a police station. There can be no hard and fast rule about it. Some de-addiction centres run by the local police department have been doing good work in Delhi. It all depends on who are the people running them and how intense and sincere is their motivation for work.

In the business sector, clinching deals over a glass of whisky has become the most common fashion. From the corporate deals, it has simmered down even to ordinary business deals entered into by private parties. That is an occasion to celebrate and what better way to do than the way it is done by the billionaires. There is no evidence to suggest that consuming hard drinks has anything to do with negotiating business deals. And yet alcoholism is spreading fast among the small entrepreneurs just because it is the 'in thing' or they have to keep up with the 'Jones'. Business executives, specially those who are very ambitious, face perpetual stress caused by chasing targets in the highly competitive world of business. For them a peg of hard drink may be just the night cap for inducing a sound sleep. When even this doesn't work there is resort to 'sleeping pills'. Barbiturates and valium are in some cases an essential component of the executive's bedroom. Gradually these people get addicted and cannot think of sleeping naturally the way the rest of the world does. Most corporate employers allow their senior executives to have membership of sports clubs or health clubs at company's cost. The company has a vested interest in the health of its executives. A healthy executive would not only perform better but also save the company the medical reimbursement bills. A game of tennis at the end of the day, some time at the golf course or a swim can be better relaxants than the sleeping pills. The awareness needs to be cultivated through a multi-media approach. The family and the society in general can contribute in their own way to ensure that the members stay out of the trap. Some enlightened employers in India have realised the importance of involving the families of their workers in the welfare programmes. Tata Iron and Steel Company (and its group of companies) and the Bharat Heavy Electricals have a very commendable track record of starting welfare programmes for the workers as well as for their families. Once engaged in purposeful activity chances of a person getting into drug net are minimal. There are many more big and small employers who have realised the importance of welfare activities like recreation clubs, centres for informal schooling, functional literacy programmes and film shows etc. where entertainment is combined with drug prevention publicity.

In cases where the incidence is relatively high, action groups formed with the purpose of prevention and drug de-addiction can be very effective. These groups could be attached to more than one institution or areas that they may visit regularly. Modest targets may be fixed for such action groups commensurate with the resources at their disposal but there must be some targets and specified responsibilities so that the programme does not become a ritual.

Such programmes are organised by the National Institute on Drug Abuse (NIDA) in USA. The programmes comprise technical assistance to business/industry on development and implementation of comprehensive programmes to keep workplaces free from drug abuse. NIDA provides consultants, publications and referral resources on drug-related subjects such as the nature and extent of drug abuse, development and enforcement of drug abuse policies, employees' education and supervisor training etc. Assistance is also provided for drug testing programmes and early detection of individuals getting into the drug net. Some of the special programmes of NIDA include:

(*a*) Operation of drug abuse information and treatment hot line. The line is tool free – the caller doesn't have to pay even for making the call.

(*b*) Distribution of drug and alcohol-related information published in research journals, magazines, videos, prevention curricula and programme descriptions.

(*c*) Development of video-tape series suitable for supervisor and employee education.

Some of the NIDA publications include

(*i*) Strategic Planning for Workplace Drug Abuse Programmes

(*ii*) Model Plan for a Comprehensive Drug-free Workplace Programme

(*iii*) Guidelines for the Development and Assessment of a Comprehensive Federal Employee Assistance Programme

(*iv*) Drug Abuse Curriculum for Employee Assistance Programme.

[*Details of the programme may be seen at Annexure A*].

Prevention at Family Level

Among the causes that lead children to drug abuse, family maladjustment stands out as one that is responsible for maximum incidence. Most addicts hail from families that do not have a normal life pattern. There seems to be a direct relationship between proneness to addiction and disturbances in normal family relationships.

It becomes necessary to analyse the family patterns before launching drug prevention programmes in any specific social group. The highly prone or risk families need to be identified as the first step. In such identified families, there would be need for improving family relationships so that their members do not get trapped into the drug trap. Prevention programmes targeted at family level are very popular in USA. These programmes are essentially based on integrated social learning approaches. These programmes usually comprise :

(*a*) *Home Visits* : Such visits are organised by 'Home-School Liaisons'. The aim is to improve communication between the teachers and the parents.

(*b*) *Parent Training Classes* : These classes are organised with a view to improving child management skills of the parents.

(*c*) *Conflict Resolution Services* : These services are intended to provide support and assistance to families that have been identified as high risk families of the social group under coverage.

The other items covered in the programmes include discussions involving the parents and the children on matters relating to drugs and drug abuse. Strategies that have to be adopted to combat the menace of children getting trapped or hooked to drugs are discussed and family rules and norms evolved.

In India and other Asiatic societies, the family bonds are more closely knit and strong as compared to those in developed societies of the West. Family interactional programmes, therefore, assume a much larger significance in India than in the West. In developed countries like USA, the addict after being treated does not go straight to his or her home. There are transit institutions that function as buffers between the de-addiction centre and the home. At the hospital, the addict is under total supervision. This supervision is relaxed in stages at halfway homes and satellite homes. At the halfway home, the patient learns to be independent partially. The medical supervision continues although not as severely as at the hospital. From here the de-addicted person moves to the satellite home where the doctors' visits are much less frequent. More freedom is allowed to the de-addicted patient. After he has gained a fair amount of confidence, he moves to his home in the final stage. Such gradual shift from hospital to home enables the de-addict to become independent in dealing with his problems and accepting the realities of life. In Indian situation, the changeover is abrupt. From the de-addiction centre, the patient goes straight to his home. In the absence of any buffer arrangements, it is necessary that the family members of the de-addicted patient are provided training in how to help him regain his confidence. The family has to provide the buffer support. So the people around must be made aware of their special role in helping the de-addicted patient to develop social skills and confidence that would once again make him a normal person.

Considering the importance of the family as an institution for moulding personality traits, it is important, and more so in traditional societies that the family structures are modified. A Persian proverb translated in English says, 'it is an offence to point out the lapses on the part of elders'. In such situations, the younger members are always hesitant to express their apprehensions or doubts. They prefer to get information from uninformed outsiders rather than their own seniors.

For proper development, the family needs to have horizontal, vertical as well as multi-interactional communication channels. Where such channels exist, the chances that boys and girls would drift into the company of drug addicts are relatively fewer. It may not be easy to provide such channels in Indian family situations. It is too much to expect that overnight a traditional Indian girl would come and confide about her infatuation for a coed with his father. But a start can be made by providing forums like T.V. where the two generations sit across the table and argue their viewpoints which may be contradictory. Parental training programmes can go a long way in modifying family structures. In so far as drug-related issues are concerned, the parents must know how to identify if the children are getting into the world of drugs. They should be told that with drugs there can be no one-time exceptions and this fact has to be drilled into the minds of the younger generation. For extreme cases, the parents must also be familiarised with how to deal with addicts. That way alone therapeutic systems can be developed and made effective.

The prevention programme has to be based on a systems approach. In this approach those sub-systems are identified which are faulty and not functioning properly. The actual restructuring is done through the agency of family counselling centres. The establishment and functioning of such centres have helped in a number of drug abuse situations. Sometimes a father may be scolding his son for drinking alcohol while he himself is an addict. The father may well say that he scolds because he knows the evils of alcohol addiction. But the son may have no regard for the advice coming from his addict father. Similar complex situations can arise when a wife is scolded or thrashed for restraining his husband from drinks or drugs. Family counselling can be the most effective agency for dealing with such situations.

It is unfortunate that in Indian situations a son would rarely go to his father even if he feels remorseful about his having taken drugs. Traditional rigidities can be extremely harmful and need to be changed lest the coming generation destroys all that has been built over the centuries.

Prevention at College Level

The school system provides close monitoring of the student activities, both in and outside the school. Schools have programmes that involve all children, both during and after the school hours. There are the curricular programmes, the co-curricular and also the extra-curricular programmes in which students function under teachers' supervision. The degree of freedom is relatively much less as compared to the environment at the college level. The school students are bound by attendance, submission of home assignments, participation in school programmes etc. exercising control over their getting wayward. But this discipline gets loosened once there is a shift to the college. The college students resent being monitered. The teachers at the college are very loosely bound to the students except in the curricular programmes. This sudden changeover from a strictly monitored to a free from controls environment makes college students most vulnerable to drugs. The risk is much higher if the student starts residing in a hostel. If he or she is on State grants, the vulnerability is further enhanced.

The first reaction of the student coming to the college is to do all that he was restrained from doing at the school. The day scholar at the college feels frustrated as he is not as free as his counterpart living in the hostel. He expresses his feeling of 'non-achievement' by rebelling at home. Even simple queries from the parents are enough to irritate him. The home no longer remains the support system it was when the student was at the school. Communications between the students and the family members start getting strained. College is the stage when the individual is in transit from adolescence to youth. Here the boys and girls have more occasions for intermixing. There are a number of questions that the youth would like to ask. But neither the parents nor the teachers can be trusted for they belong to another generation. The youth is shy and the parents feel embarrassed in answering questions their wards may like to ask. In traditional societies 'sex' cannot even be mentioned, leave aside discussions in a free and educative atmosphere.

This emotional vacuum prompts young boys and girls to turn to 'joints' where the atmosphere is free. The urban and rich boys and girls take to these joints as an expression of their rebellion against the established values of their homes which they find restrictive and obsolete. Those from rural and relatively poor families succumb to peer pressure. They do not want to be branded 'rural' or 'backward' by resisting a puff or a drink which is the in-thing.

When Shakespeare said 'Youth is wild', he summed up the mentality in just three words. Young men and women at this stage of development are so certain that nothing is going to happen to them (even when it may be happening to so many in their group). Longevity in terms of age is meaningless to them. What matters is 'today'. With this attitude they compromise to anything or everything unmindful of its long-range consequences.

Prevention programmes at the college level have to keep in mind these basic parameters. If these are ignored, the programme, howsoever idealistically conceived, will just not take off.

The prevention programmes should provide facts preferably such with which the students can identify themselves. If the students in India are fed with statistics relating to dangers of drug abuse as prevalent in USA, that would make no sense. On the other hand, if the cases referred to are those that belong to the same society, they can go a long way in instilling fear of drugs.

In trying to arouse fear of drugs, care has to be taken not to cite cases that could not come out of the net. It would be more effective if the cases dealt with and discussed are such as got into the net, lost valuable years, but came out before the final damage was done.

The programmes should involve an information sharing process. There could be group discussions in which even the extreme opinions are allowed to be expressed. If the atmosphere of such discussions is allowed to remain free, it is likely that the programme will have a perceptible impact. The experts or the resource persons present at such discussions need not counter every argument headlong, howsoever irrational it may be. The discussion should aim at presenting facts and emphasising that there are much better things that the young boys and girls are capable of than mere retreat into the world of drugs. The appeal should be to their better sense and judgement.

Altering action structure is not an easy task. More so when the group involved comprises young boys and girls. Their ego has to be respected. They have to be offered alternatives that are more in keeping with their ideals, their ambitions and their youthfully bubbling energy.

Unfortunately, there are a number of factors operating outside the college world that tend to negate the work being done against drug abuse within the campus. In Indian films, drinking is glamourised. The rich must be shown entertaining through cocktails. As said earlier, the hero drinks when he is unsuccessful. The villain drinks when he has succeeded in his clever plans. The vamp too shares a drink. The rich businessmen smoke cigars. The feudal lords smoke the traditional 'hookah' and chew tobacco. All these shows neutralise so much of what is done against drug use in the college through prevention programmes. The media pretends to support the drug abuse education by showing spots in between the programmes. These messages are very crudely put and often without regard to the viewing time or choice of the target audience. A message during a pop session could be more meaningful than between an old movie/news telecasts.

A drug prevention programme at college level may include the following :

(*a*) *Drug Prevention Centres* : These may be located in the college campus either within the college or in the hostel. These centres should organise special programmes for the newcomers guarding them against the possible designs of the drug pushers or the old addicts. It is very important that these centres do not become places where nobody would like to be seen going. A drug prevention programme that is weaved into a normal club or recreation centre would be more effective than a centre exclusively designated. A film show on drug abuse that is only a part of the total programme of the recreation centre would invite larger audience than a documentary. Similarly messages against drug abuse that form part of a total performance on the stage would be more meaningful than one exclusively and directly preaching the risks involved in the use of drugs.

(*b*) *Drug Prevention as a part of Guidance centre* : Students would like to visit a guidance centre if one exists. The centre would offer information about recruitment procedures, facilities for advanced training available in various institutions, and also provide guidance on matters like how to face interviews. If such centres have a psychologist attached, students would like to discuss their emotional hang-ups and seek solutions. Drug prevention could also be a part of the total educational and vocational guidance programme.

(*c*) *Drug Prevention through Strong Volition* : Peer pressure is a very important contributing factor in drug addiction. Young boys and girls need to be trained, to be able to say 'no' when they so feel. This training is not an easy job. But it makes all the difference between success and failure for similarly placed youth. This capacity to say 'no' is both inherent and acquired. College programmes can go a long way in helping students to acquire that capacity. Confidence-building activities go a long way in creating this capacity.

Institutions that offer a large variety of co-curricular programmes turn out students who are better equipped to say 'no'. One or two activities cannot possibly interest the large variety that enters the college. Non-participation or frequent failure in activities for which one doesn't have the competitive talents leads to demoralisation and weakening of volition. Variety of activities where each one has a fair chance of winning in one or the other reinforces self-confidence which alone is the surest guard against being driven into the world of drugs.

(*d*) *Preventing Boredom through Fewer Passive Entertainments* : So often boys and girls are driven to drugs as they feel bored. Passive entertainments like watching T.V. leave nothing to be done by the viewer. Programmes like trekking, adventure tourism, social work, participation in athletics and similar active sports keep students away from boredom. Such participation also develops a health consciousness among the participants.

While the expansion of area of personality growth would minimise the chances of students getting into the world of drugs, there would still be cases of weak personalities that may find the temptations difficult to resist. For them there would always be the need for special 'task forces'. These task forces should be given the responsibility of keeping a track on the activities of the drug pushers and the old addicts. It would be a wise policy to put the high risk identified students into the task forces. One doesn't go picking pockets once in the police uniform. Students coming out of colleges and universities are the responsibility of the society. It has to create institutions that would keep the young men and women away from the evil influence of drugs so that they are best equipped for social transformations that are the crying need of developing societies.

Cohen's Model of Prevention Programme

Level of Experience	Corresponding Motives (Examples)	Possible Alternatives (Examples)
Physical	Desire for physical satisfaction, physical relaxation, relief from sickness, desire for more energy, maintenance of physical dependency.	Athletics, dance, exercise, hiking, diet, health, training, carpentry or outdoor work.
Sensory	Desire to stimulate sight, sound, touch, taste, need for sensual-sexual stimulation.	Sensory awareness training, sky diving, experiencing sensory beauty of nature.
Emotional	Relief from psychological pain, attempt to solve personal perplexities, relief from bad mood, escape from anxiety, desire for emotional insight, liberation of feeling, emotional relaxation.	Competent individual counselling, well-run group therapy, instruction in psychology of personal development.
Interpersonal	To gain peer acceptance, to break through interpersonal barrier to "communicate," especially non-verbally, defiance of authority figures, cement two-person relationships, relaxation of interpersonal inhibition, solve interpersonal hang ups.	Expertly managed sensitivity and encounter groups, well-run group therapy, instruction in social custom, confidence training, social interpersonal counselling, emphasis on assisting others in distress via education, marriage.

8

Treatment of Drug Addicts

Drug addiction is a complex psychological and physiological behaviour pattern, and the treatment, therefore, also involves a combination of multiple strategies. The Tx programmes relate not only to the physical dependence of the addict but have to deal with multiple facets of his lifestyle. The bio-based theories believe in detoxification while the personality orientation theories emphasise re-learning behaviour patterns. Those who believe in inter-personal orientation provide a way to deal with drug addicts by altering their relationships with friends and family. Society-based theories are based on community-based support programmes.

A major problem in dealing with drug addicts through Tx is their reluctance in getting Tx. Most often the drug addicts are referred due to violent behaviour on their part or because of their suicidal tendencies. Most often the drug addicts land up in jails because of crimes committed under the influence of drugs.

Some of the techniques that have been tried successfully are being discussed in the following pages. These techniques may be tried singly or in combination, keeping in view the addict's needs, the treatment goals, the attitudes and the value system of the culture in which the addict lives and functions. Thus, the total personality and environment of the addict have to be kept in focus while deciding what strategy or combination of strategies would yield optimum results.

Psycho-dynamic Therapy

This technique deals with the root cause of the problem. Psycho-therapeutic approaches are based on a dynamic approach that takes into account the development of human behaviour as an important aspect for understanding dysfunctional behaviours. Persons with psychological problems do not understand why a certain behaviour is occurring. A 24-year-old person who has been a gold medallist during his academic career, got rejected in 25 interviews and developed nervous anxiety to the extent that he started avoiding interviews, would get fever on the day he was required to appear for interview and finally landed up with drugs. He was not able to face his parents and avoided going home. No amount of training in 'how to face interviews' could be of any help to him. During psycho-therapy sessions his problem was traced to his development being the only child of the parents who had very high expectations from him. He grew up under perpetual stress. His parents had kept him out of all activities normal for his age. The entire emphasis was that he should study so that he did well in his academic scores. All other needs emotional, psychological and even physiological were pushed to the background.

Growing up under these abnormal pressures and tensions the boy developed serious communication problems hindering his normal growth. Many of the problems that he faced as an adult were in effect a spillover from the way he had been brought up as a child.

The developmental perspective is based on stage theories of Freud, Erickson and Piaget etc. which postulate that development is inherent and takes place in predictable sequences. Obstacles in the normal development at one stage lead to problems at the later stages. Freud emphasised the role of unconscious process as determinants of psychological dysfunctions. According to him, abnormal development in oral, anal, phallic and latency stages is reflected in repression. The unhealed wounds of childhood constantly haunt behaviours in later stages of development.

Erickson's model of development is psycho-social which emphasises the role of inter-personal relationships in development. His approach is based on the whole life cycle. On the other hand, Piaget talks about the cognitive stages of development.

A person's behaviour can be seen reflected from his past the way one sees an image reflected through the mirror. Psycho-therapeutic techniques explore the basic roots of problem behaviours. The cure through such a treatment is more lasting. The person can deal with his problems that may occur in future as he learns and develops the capability to cope with them.

The drug addicts, it has been observed, have a tendency to look back into their past. The slightest provocation and they are led to remember a chain of events that had caused them pain in the past. They also relate their childhood experiences to their present behaviour. One of the commonly quoted reasons for drug use given by those suffering from depression or loneliness or with a background of having grown in a faulty family atmosphere is 'nobody cared for me'. 'I was neglected'...'I would have been so different if my parents had loved me'...In their case the addictive behaviour is self-punishing behaviour for anger towards others. If precursors of life problems are identified, the track for further future development could be laid clear.

Drug addiction is not a problem by itself. It is the reaction to some other problem faced by the user. Psycho-dynamic approaches for treatment are based on certain assumptions. They can be summarised as below :

(a) There is a conflict between suppressed impulses, feelings and thoughts that seek an expression. Psycho-therapy, specially psycho-analysis, opens up the areas of unconscious to conscious scrutiny.

(b) Psycho-therapy recognises the needs of the 'individual'. As such, the relationship between the addict client and the therapist is of immense importance. The client must have trust in the therapist. In other words, there must be a harmonious atmosphere which is conducive to the client for opening up before the therapist. Psycho-therapy sessions invariably demand an empathetic relationship that is both warm and supportive.

(c) The therapy aims at developing a positive self-concept in a drug addict. Regardless of the technique a psychotherapist adopts, it enhances a feeling of 'self-worth' in the person.

(d) Psycho-therapy provides a better understanding of self as the therapist provides a logical explanation for the present behaviour (which may be deviant). Gradually the drug addict develops an insight and starts looking at his problem in a changed and broader perspective.

(e) Free association, transference and therapeutic relationship lead to catharsis of emotions leaving the patient relieved of the intensity of his pain and sufferings.

Compared to the classical psycho-analysis techniques, the psycho-analysis-oriented therapy is more logical, practical and less time-consuming. The latter is less rigid and 'a general conversation' invariably leads to emotional release. In one case, the patient was asked to write down all his thoughts during the course of 'therapy'. The patient started with all negative observations. However, as he progressed he started being positive in his writing. The 'conversation technique' through writing had worked towards his emotional release.

Behaviour Therapy

The drug adaptive behaviour is a learned behaviour. Behaviour therapies assume that since it is a learned behaviour, it can be unlearnt through a number of techniques. The behaviour therapist is concerned with the present problems unlike the psycho-therapeutic approaches. Behaviour therapies are based on identifying antecedents and current reinforcers of maladaptive behaviour with a view to identify alternative positive reinforcers. In this 'learning orientation' the emphasis is on what particular activity of the person has to be modified. For example, while dealing with the problem of alcohol addiction, one has to keep in mind what is the quantity and frequency of drinking during the day. With these observations in mind, the habit of drinking has to be modified and ultimately checked. Behaviourists see personality as a set of various skills, abilities and capabilities that can be acquired or modified through learning.

One way to modify behaviour is to eliminate the reinforcers. Adolescents take drugs or alcohol due to peer pressure. Acceptability in the group acts as a reinforcer in such cases. If the addict can be dehooked from the existing peer group, the reinforcer would be out and it would become much easier to get the desired behaviour (no recourse to alcohol or drugs).

Systematic Desensitisation

This technique was developed by Joseph Wolpe in 1950s. The assumption behind the technique is that if a person is relaxed he cannot be anxious at that time. If people are trained to be relaxed, they could also learn how to overcome anxiety. The technique is practised in different phases.

In the first phase, the client is trained to relax the muscles and the mind. In the second phase, the anxiety-producing situations are assigned a hierarchy. Dealing with a case it was found that the addict started taking drugs after a failure in love. The patient developed a phobia so much so that he stopped talking to any girl. He developed the anxiety to go to the college as the girl was also studying at the same place. The following hierarchy of situations that used to induce anxiety in him was prepared.

The client was showing lowest anxiety on Sundays when the college was closed or on some other holiday. A high-anxiety situation was when he saw the girl moving with some other boy. The highest anxiety level was recorded when he was asked by his parents to marry some other girl. Actual desensitisation takes place in the third phase of the treatment technique. In this phase the client is made to relax in the first instance. The therapist, therefore, describes the various anxiety-producing situations. The client is asked to imagine as if he was living in the induced situation.

In the above case the lowest anxiety-inducing situation was presented to the client. The boy after being relaxed was told that the day was a holiday when he need not go to the college. The therapist observed whether the client was relaxed or not. If he was relaxed, the next situation was given to him. Thus, imagining real life situations, the patient was given practice to keep calm.

Kennedy and Kimura (1974) show that clients who progress upto 50 per cent of their anxiety hierarchy get therapeutic gains. This desensitisation technique can even be used at home, making use of a tape-recorder.

Aversion Therapy

In this therapy, the temptation for the drug (or alcohol) is curtailed by introducing aversive stimulus. It is a widely used therapy in the treatment of smokers, alcoholics and drug addicts. In ancient Rome, it was a practice to put a live eel in the wine cup with a view to inducing repulsion to the drink. These days electric shocks and several other kinds of drugs are administered to induce a feeling of nausea. A mouth wash with a very low concentration of nitrate solution after meals reduces the urge for a smoke. If a cigarette is smoked inspite of the revulsion, nausea follows.

There are certain other drugs which, if followed by alcohol, cause illness. These strategies are used to help the individual in getting over his addiction urge. The method is extremely helpful if the client is desperately willing to overcome his addiction to cigarettes or alcohol. It is also known as *deterrent therapy.* This therapy has been successfully used by the author without using any revulsion drugs but just through suggestions and auto-suggestions.

In this technique the addicts were allowed to smoke. While they were smoking, suggestions were given such as 'You are feeling choked and suffocated and not able to think properly'. Other suggestions included, 'You are having a vomitting feeling and have a bad taste in your mouth.' These suggestions were given repeatedly and in many cases the patients actually vomitted after drug use. In the second stage, they were asked to give auto-suggestions. The results were equally effective.

Punishment Technique

It is yet another way of achieving change in behaviour. In all societies trouble-makers have been punished in many ways. Scolding, social boycott, putting in jail or termination from employment are some of the well-known forms of showing social disapproval for undesirable conduct.

There is, however, a limit beyond which punishment loses its deterence. It rather provokes contra-suggestion. Beating children who smoke, admonishing employees who drink or putting in jail people who are to be found using illicit drugs has not solved the problem anywhere. At best it has led to use of drugs in a manner that the use is not easily detected till the worst damage has occurred.

Nagging invariably breeds obstinacy. In one case it was found that an 18-year boy was detected to be taking LSD by his parents. He was severely beaten and then locked up in a room for three days. The boy felt extremely humiliated and was unwilling to face people around him. He resorted to yet more deadly drugs to get over his humiliation. This time he did it so cleverly that it was not easily detectable. The whole exercise of punishment, thus, proved extremely counter- productive.

Behaviour Shaping

Behaviour shaping with positive reinforcers that do not destroy the ego of the individual is a better and effective technique. A chronic alcoholic in the company of a nagging wife is a lost case. The only hope lies in his being cared for and rewarded in his efforts to get over his habit. The praise from the wife the day her husband remains sober works as positive reinforcer. This way she can look forward to many more days of his sobriety. The theory of positive reinforcers is based on the concept that people are motivated to show those kinds of behaviour that are rewarded.

In practising such techniques, the therapist must be able to identify what reinforcers may be effective or ineffective for an individual. There can be no text-book formulas and the nature and extent of reinforcers have to be varied according to individual needs. Behaviour shaping is a technique in which addicts are taught not to escape from the situation but to face it. Confidence-building and developing a strong willpower would need plenty of initiative and originality on the part of the therapist.

Withdrawal symptoms have to be taken care of as sometimes it may take several months or years to get the desired results. Alternate behaviours are to be developed by chalking out the day schedules, goal setting etc. so that an addict may not revert to his original situations but be absorbed in the mainstream of life. Continuous vigil is necessary to achieve the desired results.

Role Modelling

Albert Bandura (1986) argued that change in behaviour may also be obtained by observing others. Social learning theorists recommend this technique for extinction of irrational fears and phobias. This technique is useful specially with those addicts who generally respond, 'I can't live without alcohol...' 'I have been taking opium since childhood. How can I leave it now ?' It is also useful with those who tried to leave their habit of chain smoking but failed. Showing a film about people who were similar addicts but are now free from addiction can be very helpful. Individuals are inclined to identify themselves with others and as such these success stories can be very meaningful and effective. Gradually the patients get a feeling that if other people could do it, why not 'I'. Personal interviews in which a chronic addict who is now free from addiction, narrates his experiences and also how he succeeded, help the patients psychologically.

Role Playing

In Role Modelling, one watches others. But in Role Playing, one has to act by himself in a certain specified role. This technique was applied in the case of a group of chain smokers. They were given a situation in which one of the clients was to act as a chain smoker and another person had to act as a therapist. Interestingly everyone wanted to act as the 'smoker'. One of the participants in the role-play was called to play the role of a smoker while the other was asked to act as the therapist. Others just watched. The smoker glamourised his smoking habits. The client who was playing the therapist failed to muster any arguments as a therapist against smoking. After this session all the participants were asked to think and plan their roles as a therapist. Gradually they developed some insight and started giving logical arguments against smoking. Later two of them were able to get rid of their habit. Through Role Playing technique, one tries to understand the other side of the picture.

In another situation, there were four clients. One of them was to act as the smoker, two as the newcomers and the fourth as the pusher. The newcomers were pressurised to have a puff. This kind of situation enables one to learn how to cope with peer pressures, how people are persuaded and pushed into the drugs net, and what are the good and polite ways of saying 'no' and also why saying 'NO' is so important.

Thus, Role Playing is also important for assertiveness training. It is a kind of rehearsal which has to be projected in real life situations later on. For those who are shy in 'speaking up', assertiveness training is very essential. They are generally the people who get influenced by other people's suggestions very easily. Assertive people generally do not submit to outside pressures, 'right' or 'wrong'. Assertiveness training can be helpful in developing pressure coping techniques among the addicts. Coleman states, "Assertive training may also be indicated in cases where an individual consistently allows other people to take advantage of him or manoeuvre him into situations which he finds uncomfortable."

This assertion is in the form of 'non-provocation' to the other person. Excessive submission leads to loss of self-esteem and increases repressed hostility.

Cognitive Therapies

These kinds of approaches are based on the presumption that beliefs determine emotions and behaviour. Irrational beliefs lead to irrational behaviour. The person who starts taking alcohol or drugs due to frequent depressive moods believes 'because I cry too much, I am worth nothing'. Others say, 'I failed in the examination because I am not intelligent. I need not live any more'. 'If I take alcohol, I will be more confident. I will then be more accepted and more successful in business.' 'People call me daring and courageous as I am capable of taking drugs.' Most drug addicts suffer from such faulty belief systems. In India, many women get into using alcohol believing that they will be recognised as modern by this behaviour. The goal for treatment in such cases is to eliminate the false beliefs and restructure the irrational thinking.

Albert Ellis evolved *Rational Emotive Therapy* (1950s). He postulated that people interpret their experiences in self-defeating manner. The therapy most of the time pinpoints the irrational beliefs. The therapist has to be active and directive. He has to tell the client about new ways of thinking.

Adler (1958) stated :

> "We don't suffer from the shock of our experiences – the so-called trauma – but we make out of them just what suits our purposes...Meanings are not determined by situations but we determine ourselves by the meanings, we give to the situations."

The modern cognitive therapists combine cognitive approach with the behavioural approach which is designed as cognitive behaviourism. It includes rational therapies, coping skill therapies and problem-solving therapies.

In modern times, when children insist on knowing the logic behind every precept, cognitive approaches are more successful. For the child who has grown with the misconception that a peg of whisky is good for digestion, it would be absurd and meaningless to be told that drinking is a bad habit. It won't satisfy him. Rational arguments will have to be given in support of the precept so that his altered logic is counteracted.

Humanistic Therapies

Therapists under this approach believe that human beings have tremendous capabilities and resources within them and, if properly cared, can have optimum psychological growth. The ultimate aim of the approach is to get self-actualisation. The approach emphasises growth and development of the individual. Roger's client therapy believes in creating a climate for change by providing positive regards to the individual and accepting him with all his strengths and weaknesses. It emphasises an empathetic relationship between client and counseller. Such a climate promotes increased self-awareness, self-worth and self-acceptance. In the words of Rogers :

> "It is that the individual has within himself or herself vast resources for self-understanding, for altering his or her self-concept, attitudes and self-directed behaviour – and that these resources can be tapped if only a definable climate of facilitative psychological attitudes can be provided (1986-P. 197)."

This sort of counselling is very helpful in dealing with drug addicts. There is a stigma attached to the addicted in most societies. They are accepted neither by their families nor by society at large. They are victims of neglect and targets of humiliation. 'He is an addict. Don't mix with him', such an attitude on the part of the society ostracises the addict and comes in the way of his reverting to the normal current of family and social life. Even after the person has come out of his addiction, he continues to be looked upon with contempt by the people around him. In such situations, many addicts revert to their pre-treatment stage. If in this otherwise hostile surroundings, the addict can get empathetic listener, where the therapist is attuned with the experiences of the addict, it goes a long way in providing him a feeling of acceptance. Therapists do not attach any value judgements and as such the addicts find it easy to confide in the therapist. They come out with what they think and also why they act in a particular manner in a given situation.

"If clients can see that someone else believes in their capacity to grow, they may begin to believe in themselves" (Meador and Rogers, 1984). The role of the therapist is that of an active listener. Crooks and Stein wrote:

> "The therapist, in effect, tries to get 'under the skin' of the client to the point where the therapist may be aware even of the feelings or meanings that the client is not yet aware of."

The author has successfully tried this technique in dealing with drug abusers and alcoholics in Indian situations where the society is passing through the transitional stage from a strong joint family to a nuclear system. In the nuclear family there is no time for people to be together and share their thoughts and feelings, such is the demand of modernity. Children feel neglected as the parents, often both of them working, have a very busy schedule for the day and are too tired in evening. In such situations there arises the need for counselling.

Another spokesman of the humanistic approach is Fredrick Perls (1948, 1973). He believes that a therapist must be active, directive and also manipulative to encourage self-reliance, and self-awareness. He opines that all parts of self, *i.e.,* 'wholeness' are important. Problems arise when one is not able to integrate all parts of the personality including cognition, affection and connotation. The therapist helps the individual to integrate his disintegrated self. Role playing technique (discussed earlier) which is commonly used by Gestalt theorists has been helpful in treating drug addicts.

Several other techniques are followed in the one-to-one relationship. The objective is to help the client to take out his hidden thoughts to 'here and now' experiences by pointing out what therapist observes. One alcoholic client began his narration thus: 'Some people take alcohol because...' The therapist asked him to talk in terms of first person. As the client started talking, 'I take alcohol because' he had started owning his feelings. Non-verbal clues are pointed out by the therapist if there are any discrepancies in what the client is saying and what he is feeling. The following is one example.

Client : No... No... I don't take drugs (He says it with his eyes lowered and voice stammering)

Counsellor : Are you sure ?

Client : With a pause Yh...

Counsellor : Then why do you stammer. Why don't you look into my eyes and say so ?

Client keeps mum.

Counsellor : Face me and say that.

Thus by pointing out the non-verbal clues, the client gradually becomes able to accept the real feelings and thoughts.

Systems Approaches

The systems approaches of treatment are based on the concept that the individual is interacting with several systems and sub-systems at the same time. The systems are inter-related. Problems arise when one or more of the systems become dysfunctional. The treatment, therefore, lies in making that system/sub-system functional.

These systems/sub-systems in the case of an individual may be the family, the school, the community or the society. While discussing the causes of drug addiction, it was emphasised that faulty family patterns or pressures from peer groups often lead to a person becoming a drug addict. In such cases treating the person alone will not serve the purpose. Since the person has to revert to his system, there is need for treating the system which may be the family or the peer group.

The Family Therapy

The drug abusive behaviour may be projection of the internal conflict arising out of lack of proper communication and interactions within the family. In one case, the father's extra- marital relationship induced in his son a self-destructive behaviour. He started taking drugs to show his hostility towards his father. His logic was that since my father loves me, he will feel tortured when he knows of my drug use. Yet another situation may be where a husband is driven to drugs because of 'not so caring' or perpetually nagging wife. In the Family Therapy, the entire family is treated as 'a client'. The aim of the therapy in such cases is to redefine the role of each family member. The final desired outcome is a harmonious system of inter-relationships.

Family Therapy is very popular in Europe and other developed societies in the USA. However, when we consider the prevailing value systems in India, the effectiveness of Family Therapy is conditioned by many peculiarities.

In most families, there is just one 'decider'. He may be the father or the living grandfather in case of joint families. All children and juniors are taught to obey and obedience without arguing is considered the highest virtue. Defiance of parental authority is a near sin. In this situation multi-channel communication system does not work. In such cases it is very difficult for the therapist to tell the decider that he is in the wrong. The usual answer would be, "I have seen life, I am the father and I know what is best for my children." The elder member of the family would hardly ever accept that his behaviour has been responsible for driving his son into the world of drugs.

The family decider is always correct in such situations. It is the other person who is responsible for whatever bad happens to the members of the family. *Couple Therapy* (where both the partners are called for therapy) has been tried in Indian conditions where the husband happens to be an alcoholic or a drug addict. It has been observed that socialisation process ascertains the gender roles in the community. In societies that are male-dominated, *Couple Therapy* is not without risks. The women in such societies are expected to show a certain kind of behaviour, that is, tolerance and subordination to the male. Women are reluctant to participate in Couple Therapy for more than one reason. In one case it was found that after the session, the wife was rebuked for having exposed his husband to outsiders and, thus, humiliated him. In such situations, it is more desirable that both partners are tackled separately. Family or Couple Therapies have to be administered with great care in such situations.

Group Therapy

There are occasions when people say, 'Why not me' ? These occasions may be related to great achievements of life that somebody had. But there are also occasions when people think 'Why only me' ? These situations may be feeling tense or frustrating because of having been ignored in the reward for a work done. In the second situation, the person is put in a group of persons who have similar problems. In their presence the frustrated person gets some relief in the thought that such things do not happen to him alone. The drug-addict who gets a severe craving due to non-availability of drugs finds it difficult to cope with the situation. But when he is made to interact with persons similarly placed or deprived, he develops within him an insight that helps him in coping with the deprivation. He also becomes less reluctant to accept that he is a drug addict since such acceptance does not put him as the odd man of the group. In such cases group therapies have an upper hand as compared to individual therapies. These are also less time consuming as addicts are treated in a group.

In Group Therapy programmes, psycho-drama and role-playing techniques discussed earlier are used effectively. The therapy may include activities such as organising group discussions on topics relating to drug abuse. Coleman writes about the 'Didactic group therapy' in which formal lectures and visual materials are presented to a group of clients. Film show followed by a group discussion may provide the base for further treatment of the addicts.

Self-Help Groups

In societies where support systems such as family or peer group have failed in helping the individual, self-help groups have emerged to provide a helping hand to the distressed. Alcoholics Anonymous (AA) and the Narcotics Anonymous (NA) are such self-help groups that are very popular in USA. These groups provide a very different perception to the problem. Such groups have formed 12 steps known as statements of belief. These are as follows :

Steps of Alcoholics Anonymous

1. We admitted we were powerless over alcohol — that our lives had become unmanageable.
2. Came to believe that a Power greater than ourselves could restore us to sanity.
3. Made a decision to turn our will and our lives over to the care of God *as we understood Him.*
4. Made a searching and fearless moral inventory of ourselves.
5. Admitted to God, to ourselves, and to another human being the exact nature of our wrongs.
6. Were entirely ready to have God remove all these defects of character.
7. Humbly asked Him to remove our shortcomings.
8. Made a list of all persons we had harmed, and become willing to make amends to them all.
9. Made direct amends to such people wherever possible, except when to do so would injure them or others.
10. Continued to take personal inventory and when we were wrong promptly admitted it.
11. Sought through prayer and meditation to improve our conscious contact with God *as we understood Him,* praying only for knowledge of His will for us and the power to carry that out.
12. Having had a spiritual awakening as the result of these steps, we tried to carry this message to alcoholics, and to practise these principles in all our affairs.

Steps of Narcotics Anonymous

1. We admitted we were powerless over addiction — that our lives had become unmanageable.
2. Came to believe that a Power greater than ourselves could restore us to sanity.
3. Made a decision to turn our will and our lives over to the care of God *as we understood Him.*
4. Made a searching and fearless moral inventory of ourselves.
5. Admitted to God, to ourselves, and to another human being the exact nature of our wrongs.
6. Were entirely ready to have God remove all these defects of character.
7. Humbly asked Him to remove our shortcomings.
8. Made a list of all persons we had harmed, and become willing to make amends to them all.
9. Made direct amends to such people wherever possible, except when to do so would injure them or others.
10. Continued to take personal inventory and when we were wrong promptly admitted it.
11. Sought through prayer and meditation to improve our conscious contact with God *as we understood Him,* praying only for knowledge of His will for us and the power to carry that out.
12. Having had a spiritual awakening as the result of these steps, we tried to carry this message to other addicts and to practice these principles in all our affairs.

Traditions of Narcotics Anonymous

We keep what we have only with vigilance, and just as freedom for the individual comes from the Twelve Steps, so freedom for the group springs from our traditions. As long as the ties that bind us together are stronger than those that would tear us apart, all will be well.

1. Our common welfare should come first, personal recovery depends on N.A. unity.
2. For our group purpose there is but one ultimate authority— a loving God as He may express Himself in our group conscience. Our leaders are but trusted servants, they do not govern.
3. The only requirement for membership is a desire to stop using.
4. Each group should be autonomous except in matters affecting other groups of N.A. as a whole.
5. Each group has but one primary purpose — to carry the message to the addict who still suffers.
6. An N.A. group ought to have never endorsed, financed, or lent the N.A. name to any related facility or outside enterprise, lest problems of money, property or prestige divert us from our primary purposes.
7. Every N.A. group ought to be fully self-supporting, declining outside contributions.
8. Narcotics Anonymous should remain forever non-professional, but our service centres may employ special workers.
9. N.A., as such, ought to have never organised, but we may create service boards or committees directly responsible to those they serve.
10. Narcotics Anonymous has no opinions on outside issues; hence the N.A. name ought to have never drawn into public controversy.
11. Our public relations policy is based on attraction rather than promotion; we need always maintain personal anonymity at the level of press, radio, and films.
12. Anonymity is the spiritual foundation of all our traditions, ever reminding us to place principles above personalities.

These groups are active in India in cities like Bangalore, Panaji, Madras, Secundrabad, New Delhi, Cochin, Mangalore, Nagpur, Pune and Mysore.

Voluntary organisations (also referred to as NGOs) play a very important role in promoting the cause of de-addiction. A list of such organisations, de-addiction centres and After Care Homes is available in Annexure B of the book. Seva Dham in Bombay is a unique centre in the sense that it is being run by an ex-addict.

Several other groups have been working in India and abroad at the community level. Some countries have developed 'Therapeutic Communities' which are residential institutions dealing with addicts/criminals. These institutions engage the inmates in productive activities besides treatment.

Medical Treatments

Alcohol

(*i*) Sometimes minor tranquillizers are given to make alcoholics sleep. Most of the times it doesn't help because the person develops an alternate dependency on the tranquillizer.

(*ii*) Intra-muscular injections of emetine hydrochloride are given. The addict is offered alcohol after the injection. The effect is nausea and retching just at the sight and smell of alcohol. Gradually it is associated to aversion to the habit of taking alcohol. Extremely uncomfortable effects are also created if disulpherim is followed with alcohol consumption.

Opium and its derivatives

Methadone treatment is provided to opiate/heroin addicts. Methadone is a synthetic narcotic analgesic which is administered to patients as a substitute for heroin in smaller amounts for gradual physical withdrawal from opiate dependence. Other medicines that are used for detoxification of opiate addicts include diphenoxylate and propoxiphene. Doctors argue that narcotic antagonists such as cyclozocine and naltrexone are better than methadon treatment as these are not self-addicting, and, therefore, cannot be abused.

Barbiturates

The withdrawal symptoms in barbiturate addicts are lessened by giving small doses of barbiturates itself.

Hallucinogens, LSD etc.

Hospitalisation, sometimes for long periods, is required in such cases.

Doctors also prescribe some other anti-depressants and tranquillizers to treat the drug addicts. Medicinal treatment need to be followed by behaviour modification therapies to get desired results. Medicines can at best control physical dependence. For psychological dependence, psycho-therapy and other techniques are essential. In all cases the medicines should be taken on the doctor's prescription and under his monitoring care. Dr. Sharma from Agra College, Agra, suggested certain herbal combines with multiple vitamins as helpful in the treatment of drug addicts.

Homoeopaths claim to treat the withdrawal symptoms of drug addicts through use of medicines like rhus tox, aconite, nux vomica and other combinations of bio-chemic medicines. The Chinese accupunture has also been tried by some experts for treatment of drug addicts with some measure of success.

Yoga, with its technique of meditation, offers mental relaxation leading to ultimate drug de-addiction. Since it has its roots in India and enjoys a great measure of respectability, social as well as religious, it is very much suitable for Indian conditions. Yogic meditation is the practice of deliberatly altering consciousness in an effort to achieve a state of tranquillity, relaxation and inner peace (Crooks and Stein, 1988).

Meditation is a technique of concentration on a single stimulus or sound or image. It is linked to a range of physiological changes. Studies have shown that meditators exhibit alpha brain waves which are characteristic of a relaxed state of mind. Meditation programmes have been used in clinical settings successfully to reduce drug/alcohol dependency. (Kanellakos, 1978, Raskin *et al*, 1980).

If the most modern societies need the wisdom of the most ancient civilisations, one can only say, "The wheel has gone full circle".

Some Japanese therapies known as Marita therapy and Naikan therapy for relaxation may also be used for treating drug addicts. In the Marita therapy clients are expected to maintain a diary and to write about their feelings towards incidents that occur in daily routine. The therapist after reviewing these asks patients to locate purpose; accept their feelings and control behaviour. Any symptomatic reaction such as anxiety is accepted. The therapy is based on the Buddhist conviction that the way out of suffering is to give up selfish attachments and shift attention to work (K. Smith, 1981).

Naikan therapy "emphasises guided self-reflection, but the significant aim is to produce a guilt about what one has done and at the same time a sense of being cared for despite one's inadequacies. The objective is to move the client from obsessive selfishness to a gratitude for daily supports and a willingness to help others – a shift from self-concern to concern for others". Naikan therapy is a way to assault one's own self-image leading to evaluate oneself with a different frame of mind.

A number of techniques may be used singly or in combination to treat the drug abusers/addicts. The most important thing, however, is to penetrate deep into the problem and treat the root cause. Superficial cures mostly lead to relapse. The goals of intervention must be very clear and specific and should be based on the needs of the individual. During treatment programmes the social perspective must also be kept in mind. The psychological development of the individual must, however, remain in the focus.

10

Life Skill Training Through Self-help Techniques

The individual's environment plays a very decisive role in driving him into the drug addiction net and also in helping him stay out of it when exposed to identical temptations. Programmes aimed at prevention of drug abuse have, as such, to target the environment and circumstances that are responsible for the damage.

While accepting that environment plays a crucial role, it is equally relevant that in the last analysis it is the individual's self-structure, the will-power and confidence which determines whether or not a person would fall a victim or be able to withstand the drug temptation.

It is common experience that two persons exposed to similar circumstances do not necessarily react in similar ways. There are some who have learnt to cope with failures in life and have their own stress coping strategies. When faced with challenges, some persons accept defeat too soon and resort to shortcuts or just withdraw from the situation. On the other hand, there are others fired by ambition, intense desire to face challenges and a positive attitude to life which helps them to achieve inspite of failures. They are more confident about their worth, have a higher self-esteem and a thought pattern that is so different from those who prefer to retreat at the first sign of failure.

'I took drugs because I am not cared at home.' That's a very frequently offered excuse by children when face-to-face with the counsellor. But everyone who 'is not cared' does not start taking drugs. Most others develop their own coping strategies to deal with the problem. Drugs are no panacea for failures, or disasters, big or small.

No storm ever vanish just because some people choose to close their eyes or like the ostrich bury their heads in sand. Storms have (*i*) *Testing Personal Control*

The treated addict often is tempted to take a 'glass of whisky' or a puff feeling overconfident that since he has been treated once, such minor indulgence is not going to take him back. This is a misconception and can be extremely harmful. The treated addict has to scrupulously avoid any indulgence, howsoever small.

(*ii*) *Non-acceptance in the Social Mainstream*

The addict gets a stigma in the society. So even after he has been cured, people avoid his company. Sometimes fingers may be raised, there may be 'hiss hiss' at other times, as he moves around. Parents may warn their children to be away from him since he was, once, an addict. Such behaviour on the part of the society breaks the morale of the liberated addict. In desperation he feels like going back to his original stage where he used to be socially accepted.

(*iii*) *Dealing with Craving*

In certain cases, upto two years after the treatment, the craving for the drug persists. During de-addiction programmes, the addict feels that his craving for drugs is over but most of the times it gets suppressed. These suppressed feelings try to come up in more than one situation. Sometimes a person may dream that he is back with his old friends of the drug circle. As he wakes up, his craving would be intense. Similar intensity of craving can develop in moods of depression or anxiety disorders. These situations need to be guarded, both by the addict and those supervising his rehabilitation.

(*iv*) *Temptation to go back to the Drug Users' Company*

The treated addict often misses the company of his old drug-friends. He may like to visit them again just to say 'Hello'. But this type of visit can be very dangerous. The suggestion from any of his old friends to have a puff at least for company's sake could take him back to drugs.

(*v*) *Sudden Availability of Cash*

The treated addict must be given big cash handling with great care for sometime. Once he is flush with cash, his first urge would be to have a puff or a drink, something he has missed for so long.

(*vi*) *Coping with Negative Feelings*

The drug addict, unlike the normal person, knows only one way of expressing his feelings. He drinks to celebrate and also drinks when dejected. In the de-addiction programme, he has to be trained to express normal human feelings of anger, guilt, sorrow or happiness the way everyone else does. If he knows no other way, the danger is that he may relapse when exposed to situations not foreseen.

(*vii*) *Use of Prescribed Medicines*

Follow-up of the treatment is a very important component in taking the addict permanently out of the drug craving. Thus, even medicines that contain 'drugs' have to be avoided by the treated addict. For example, 'codeine' is a drug to which some people get addicted. Some medicines for cough contain this drug although in small percentages. But the treated patient has to be kept away from such minimal doses as may contain the medicine.

(*viii*) *Boredom*

The drug addict can while away all the time at his disposal just lying around. Once de-addicted, there is time which has to be filled by purposeful activity. In the absence of purposeful activity, the treated addict will get bored which can drive him back to his original status.

So often the person de-addicted from alcohol starts using tobacco. The smoker may stop smoking but start chewing tobacco. This is only self-deception. Out of smoking but back to chewing the same hardly has any meaning. Both the treating doctors and the family members supervising him at home should take special care to keep the treated patients out of substitutes equally dangerous.

Prevention of Relapse

The goal of prevention of relapse is to initially make drugs psychologically not acceptable to the treated addict. Physical non-availability alone would not be enough. It is true that drug use is possible only if drugs are available, but non-availability of drugs is only an ideal situation. The effort should be to strengthen the psychological mechanism that would keep the person out of temptation. The following methods may be adopted for prevention of relapse.

Identification of Risk Situations

As in the case of prevention programmes for drug abuse, the first important thing is to identify the situations which may promote relapse. Information has to be collected with regard to the client's past associates, his fantasies and similar high-risk behaviours. All these risk situations have to be guarded against very carefully.

Relapse Rehearsals

These have to be conducted during the de-addiction treatment itself. Before being sent home, the patient should be exposed to risk situations and efforts have to be made to reinforce his internal control mechanism. He should not be declared treated until such mechanism against possible relapse has been developed to some satisfactory level.

Follow-up and Resocialisation

It is quite likely that the addict lost all his old friends once he got into the drug group. Now that he is out, efforts should be made to get him accepted in the mainstream of the society preferably by his old friends who are best placed to keep him purposefully employed as well as socially accepted.

Misconceptions

During counselling sessions with cigarette smokers, the author found a relationship between stress and relapse and also between creative activities and relapse. The risk of relapse was found to be much higher in case of smokers who associated smoking with stress relaxation. Similarly students who believed that smoking helped them to concentrate better or create original things had a much higher tendency to relapse. Their favourite arguments or justifications for reverting to smoking were that they could not stand mental stress without smoking or that new ideas did not come to them unless they smoked cigarettes. These misconceptions are to be taken care of.

Motivational Reinforcement

In some cases the reason behind leaving a drug may not be individual motivation or inner will but compulsions such as pressure from a family member, social group, fear of losing the job, divorce or some other punishments. In such cases the fear loses its intensity after some time. The drug euphoria returns back and becomes prominent once again. In such cases relapse occurs.

In other cases it has been observed that initially the individual is motivated to be absent from drugs, gradually this motivation decreases, as Saunders and Allsuop (1987) has pointed out, 'enthusiasm for abstinence may decay overtime'.

In such cases it is necessary to reinforce the motivational factors so that relapse does not occur.

The relapse prevention programme should ensure total acceptance of the de-addict in his normal social group. This would involve training programmes for the spouse, or/and parents so that they know how to behave with the treated addict to ensure that he doesn't go back on the track.

Prevention of Mood Disorders

The addicts who suffer from mood disorders and have a history of getting attacks of deep depressions are more susceptible for relapse (Munoz's *et al* 1989). Programme of depression prevention or intervention is helpful in decreasing negative moods upto one year after treatment in persons with high rate of depression.

Multiple Drug Users

'For individuals whose use of a specific drug has been linked to other drugs, total abstinence from all drugs may be necessary.' Sharon M. Hall, David A. Wasserman, Barbara E. Havassy (1991).

Researches show that alcohol consumption is an important precursor to cocaine relapse.

The phenomenon of relapse is important as it negates all efforts made towards de-addiction. It is, therefore, necessary that measures to de-addict and prevent relapse are enforced with equal concern.

9

The Psychology of Relapse

Billions of dollars are being spent all over the world towards de-addiction of drug abusers. However, the de-addicted person is not always able to maintain his *status quo*. He finds it very difficult to live with behavioural changes that had crept into his psyche as a result of drug de-addiction. The treatment programme helps him but only temporarily in most cases. The relapse rate has been found to be as high as 80 per cent in case of addicts who seem to have been cured at one stage.

The phenomenon of relapse is no less dangerous than addiction. While addiction causes helplessness, relapse reinforces the individual's feeling for lack of confidence in himself. This is a more pathetic syndrome since even while in treatment, the addict is haunted with the fear that he would in course of time relapse into his pre-treatment stage. He starts believing that 'I just cannot do without drugs'. This fear of relapse keeps the addict away from the de-addiction programme. Once relapsed to pre-de-addicted situation his mind gets totally burnt out with the apprehension that if he again goes for treatment he would again be in the original addiction trap. This situation prevents an addict even to report for treatment.

It seems that de-addiction treatment and programmes are not complete in themselves. Once the craving for drugs has been put under control, the addicts are sent back to their homes. It is at this stage that the addicts need confidence-building exercises. These individuals need to be gradually made self-reliant so that they can withstand the temptations of going back to drugs without any external supervision. It is the success of these self-confidence-building exercises that would ultimately decide whether the treatment has been successful in giving a permanent reprieve or not. A number of causes are responsible for the relapse other than insufficiency of treatment programmes. Some have been identified as follows:

to be faced. If a person has started taking drugs that's not the end of the road. The drug abuser can help himself in a number of ways. Many of the techniques discussed in the following pages can be attempted with success.

But before that, there is the need for understanding and appreciating that the ideal conditions just do not exist anywhere in any society. There have been shortcomings. Some people have known only one way of surviving those imperfections resort to drugs.

It is too much to expect that some day with all efforts that mankind has been making, the world would be totally drug-free. It is only human to have dreams but it is equally natural that many a dreams fall short of reality. This gap between the dream and the reality can be responsible for widely varying consequences. It could prompt a person to work harder till success is achieved. It may be the occasion for. analysis of past efforts. It could also be the starting of some negative attitudes to life.

The suggestions that have been discussed below have worked successfully with many persons with whom the author had contacts during counselling sessions. These people had taken drugs occasionally or very frequently at some stage.

Coping with Loneliness

The feeling of loneliness stands out as a major cause for drug addiction. Surprisingly, the reason operates both in highly industrialised societies as also in traditional Asian societies. It would be fair to argue that loneliness by itself is independent of the stage of economic development of the society.

There can be no strict rules about how and when a person could feel lonely. Marital status does not play a determining role. A person can feel lonely even within his own family. Singles could be both lonely and without that feeling if they have a purpose and commitment to a specific cause. Researches into behaviours of drug addicts from amongst college students have shown that many addicts move frequently in social groups. A feeling of loneliness could, therefore, not be the contributing factor for drug addiction in their case. But further analysis in this area has revealed that the loneliness that seems contributory is different from being together at the physical level. What is often lacking among the inmates of formal groups is interaction at the emotional level. The associations are superficial making people lonely even when in the company of 'friends'. The inner world of thoughts, emotions and feelings remains untouched leading to a feeling of loneliness even when people are in company.

Once this difference between being in a group just physically and reacting with the group at emotional levels has been perceived, it becomes much easier to cope with this phenomenon. The remedy lies in overcoming the self-imposed artificiality of relationships.

There are many compulsions that are responsible for this aloofness even while one lives in a group. It could be so-called 'formality' as the accepted code of conduct. In big cities it is considered uncivilised to feel concerned about matters relating to the neighbours. So people live in 'group housing colonies' but totally cut off from the 'group'.

The practical suggestion for coping with artificiality of behaviour is to identify friends with whom one has some common areas of interest. Friendly relationships should be extended so that there is association in common pursuits over and above formal relationship. Such interactions would break the feeling of loneliness and give purpose to life whereafter withdrawal from life would no longer appeal as an alternative.

One person has to start. There are many others who feel similarly and would be too willing to join.

Introspection

This involves self-analysis or moving in the 'inner world'. This 'inner world' may be developed into a 'logical world' by organising haphazard thoughts and feelings through a conversation with the 'self'. If this 'inner self' is developed into a logical structure, it would be acceptable both to the individual and the society. Impartial self-analysis leads to shifting of actions that are not desirable and must not be repeated. By introspection, one learns to accept his own weaknesses. Once these are known, one can think of ways and means to overcome them. Where an alcoholic analyses how and why he started taking alcohol, he would be able to find out what other possible strategies could have been adopted to meet the situations rather than running away from them through alcohol consumption. That could be the starting of the will to try other options rather than continuing with alcoholism.

The 'Guilt' Feelings

Most people live with a feeling of guilt for having done something in the past either against their conscience or against the accepted norms of the society. They do not have the courage to accept the fact of their having committed those acts. This continued living with the feeling of guilt develops a number of complexes in personality. The insecurity that follows distorts the personality. In cases, where an addict feels he is resorting to drugs because that helps him getting over his feelings of guilt, the best thing is to talk it over. The individual, when he talks, about his fear or guilt feels 'light'. It is something like a 'confession'.

When such 'talking' is done in groups it helps the individual by way of feeling that he is not the only one to have acted in a particular manner. There are many more who are in the same boat. His acts may be very normal for his age. A person who has taken drugs once or more often feels that he has committed a sin. But when he knows there are other persons too who have tried drugs at some time, the feeling of guilt is reduced. The important thing is not to brood over the past but to get out of it. Professional psychologists can play a very determining role in counselling such cases. Even friends and relations in whom the individuals have trust can be very helpful.

To give a specific example, in India, 'virginity' in respect of women is considered pious and sex out of wedlock is a sin, both for men and women. Quite a significant number of persons suffer from sex guilt feelings. This category also includes persons who are victims of such acts. The sense of guilt in the victim is no less than that in the victimiser unless the latter has been hardened.

Others who suffer from a feeling of guilt are persons who only think about unsocial acts or vices without actually committing them. In all such cases there is need for an end to this self torturing exercise. These situations should be talked over rather than brooded over a glass of alcohol or a puff of some drugs. On most occasions, people who resort to drugs to escape the feeling of guilt are those who do not have the courage to accept their having committed certain acts that did not conform to their family or social norms. For all such people there may be others waiting to heed and help. Hence the need to talk it out.

Setting the Goals of Life

"I belong to a family of doctors. My two brothers and one sister are doctors. Both my parents are doctors. Once, I was rehearsing for a school drama. My father said, 'Why are you wasting your time in these foolish things? Aspire for the medical profession." Since that day I set my goal to be a doctor. I worked hard but could not get through the medical entrance examination. I started feeling that people at home treated me with sarcasm. I had nothing left in life. I used to cry for hours together sitting alone in my room with the doors shut from within." The boy with the above narration finally got trapped in drugs.

An analysis of the case shows that neither the boy could set proper goals for himself nor his family members gave him the right direction to set goals in life. The important thing is to set goals that are realistic and capable of achievement. There should be short-term goals as also long-term goals. Apart from the main goal one must also have alternate goals so that he may not 'collapse' if his projections do not come true in the earlier stages of effort.

Most drug addicts are people with no specific commitments or purpose in life. Once a person has something positive to work for and look forward to in life, keeping away from drugs is much more easier. The idle brain is most likely to drift into undesirable alleys.

Dare to Dream

Most people think that dreams never come true. When they are unable to achieve what they had dreamt, they feel it's the end of everything for them. This is not the whole truth. Prejudices and pre-conceived notions about things are the greatest barriers to a smooth course in life. The dreams are in themselves intoxicating and one need not resort to drugs to get high. One who can dream can feel high even without recourse to drugs or alcohol. Of course, one has to strive to make the dreams come true. For that, life has to be filled with a variety of activities. These activities should be chosen depending on individual interests. The targets have to be set for the year and then broken into the month. A further sub division would be necessary so that there is a small target for the day which would ultimately lead to the larger target. Hence, it is important to dream for the day and pursue with planned action and a strong will-power to make it come true. The dream for the day, when achieved, will give a feeling of achievement that puts one much higher than the drug or alcohol. People who dream have no time to get bored. Researches on children have established that those who do not dream often turn violent. In adolescent cases, those who become aggressive and abuse drugs/alcohol are mostly those who lacked a rich fantasy life.

Counting Small Achievements

Big achievements happen just once or twice in life. It is the small achievements which we so often ignore as of little consequence that make life pleasant and colourful. One has to learn to count the small achievements and feel happy about them. The intensity of pain is deeper and lasts for a longer period than the intensity of happiness The general tendency is to forget the happy moments, bow down to atrocities of life, always looking for something great to happen. That way one misses so much of happiness that comes around everyday. Those who aspire to be out of the drug net may start searching happy moments that they pass through everyday. Feeling happy is a state of mind and mind should be trained to count the blessings howsoever small.

Concern for Others

No drug in the world can make a person as high as the joy of sharing and caring. Once a person learns to help people in distress, he would be the recipient of so much contentment that there would be no need for drugs to get a feeling of being high. The addict can just start with asking another person of his drug group to get out of the drugs. Once such an argument and persuasion starts, it will also have a sobering effect on the user counsellor ultimately leading to self-reform.

Practise Saying 'NO'

One doesn't cope with life perpetually living under the fear that put in an adverse situation, there would have to be recourse to drugs. Life situations have to be faced and for that one has to develop the capacity to say 'No' when needed. This capacity to say 'no' builds up self-confidence and self-esteem.

The very first step could be a decision to say 'NO' when a drink/cigarette or a drug is offered. The decision has to be backed by introspective analysis as to why one has to say 'NO'. If the habit is an old one, it may not be cured in one day. In such cases the decision may be 'I shall not smoke on two fixed days of the week' Once this routine has been adhered to, the number of days can be increased. This kind of assertiveness training may be practised through self-assertion. There are also groups all over the world that provide this kind of training. Details of these kinds of groups have been discussed in the chapter on treatment.

Explore the Support System

Believe it, everybody needs a shoulder to cry on. It has to be searched. The search for a support system could be from amongst the family members with whom there is proper communication and mutual trust. In case there is not much that the family could offer, one has to go for other 'human relationships'. There could be the teacher, the friend, the doctor, the psychologist or any other person with whom mutual confidence and trust exists. It has been established through researches that drug abuse is a kind of 'defensive' behaviour. In the absence of any human support system one finds drugs / alcohol as his psuedo – 'support system' which in reality is self-deception.

Laughter, the Best Medicine

Each one of us possesses the talent to laugh and make others laugh. The talent needs to be nurtured in some cases while in others it comes naturally. Humour can occur in the normal course or even may have to be contrived. Laughter is a kind of releaxing exercise for the body and the mind.

Drug abusers who are in the process of leaving the habit often get relapse. They express themselves in two ways. When they say, 'I got relapsed' either they feel guilty that they could not maintain de-addiction or they simply laugh it over saying 'Oh yarr, I didn't drink for months. Last week one of my friends visited my home with a bottle of beer. It was nice weather and I couldn't resist.'

People who can laugh over their follies can overcome their evil habits much more easily. They can analyse their behaviour in a relaxed mood. On the other hand, persons who feel guilty and brood, soon start feeling 'I cannot do it'. Laughing over one's failures gives the strength to try again and not to give up at just one failure. Laughing heals up emotional damage. One can overcome several complexes, stresses and anxieties if one has learnt to smile and laugh.

The capacity to laugh could be cultivated through external stimulus in case there isn't enough of it within. One could read comics, watch comedies or even go through cartoons to develop the sense of humour.

Dr. Glenn Wilson has classified humour in the following five categories :

(*i*) *Aggressive Humour* : It is directed towards some one transforming them into laughable victims.

(*ii*) *Sexual Humour* : It allows us to feel relaxed about topics that make people anxious.

(*iii*) *Social Humour* : It can smoothen relations between groups, reinforce group cohesiveness or, as in case of political satire, try to influence our perception of social realities.

(*iv*) *Intellectual Humour* : It allows us momentary freedom from the tyranny of logical thinking by allowing us to play with words and concepts. Nonsense humour and puns are good examples.

(*v*) *Defensive Humour* : It can be black humour, making fun of frightening things such as cancer, bad accidents and death.

The rule is to disarm yourself from tensions and guilt through practising any type of humour and you will find yourself a changed man.

Inculcating a Relaxing Life-style

If drugs are used for relaxing from day-to-day stress it does not really work. One gets used to a certain dose and thereafter it doesn't calm any further. The hangover prompts one to have some more and drug for relaxation soon becomes a 'self-defeating strategy'. Fatigue and tiredness are also caused by lack of activity or passive activities like just watching T.V. A relaxing lifestyle would be developed through techniques such as :

1. *Meditation*

It develops concentration and helps in taming the wandering thoughts, thus making the mind and the body calm and relaxed.

2. *Muscular relaxation*

It involves identifying the behaviour, voice, tone, music, word or person that is associated with relaxation. Resort to such behaviour turns down internal tension.

3. *Imaginative relaxation*

Close the eyes and think about things that make you happy.

4. *Deep breathing*

The tired system needs greater oxygen supply to come to normal. Deep breathing helps. It should be practised with the body and the mind let loose.

5. *Massage*

Warm water massage accelerates blood circulation. Toxins that develop when one works hard are removed faster as the affected body parts are given a warm massage.

6. *Trigger Identification*

Certain triggers drive to drinks or drugs. Relaxing techniques should be used when such a trigger appears. While relaxing, one should suggest that drugs don not help. They just postpone problems. One has to become immune to the trigger that induces temptations to take drugs. Gradually there will be association of relaxation with situations that produce drug-related behaviour. Conditional response to taking drugs will be replaced by, 'Keeping Calm'.

Developing Internal Locus of Control

Those who have confidence in shaping their lifestyles in their own ways are governed by internal locus of control. On the other hand, those who depend too much on others submit to external controls easily. The drug abusers have to be internally strong to get over their problems, otherwise they will be slaves of circumstances and daily life situations. The drug abuser would always say, 'It was so destined to happen'. They don't believe in self-power. They may develop their self-power by repeatedly suggesting that, 'destiny is in their hands'.

Developing Consciousness of Changes

Each one of us has to be conscious of certain inevitable changes that occur as one grows in age. Certain very important physical and personality changes take place as one steps into adolescence. Similarly, changes take place when one grows into adulthood. One needs to be familiar with these changes. Adult roles involve certain positive modifications. One has to act more responsibly. It would be wrong to identify adulthood with just the freedom to smoke or take alcohol. Drugs do not symbolise adulthood. This should be distinctly understood.

Nurturing Creativity

It is a common misconception that the use of drugs promotes creativity. It is unfortunate that most creative artists, musicians, composers, literary persons like poets and authors resort to drugs under the belief that the best of them comes out only when they are 'high'. Drugs destroy the personality of the artist and in this process the creativity. The classical artists who practised for long years under the guidance of their 'gurus' achieved excellence through 'Riyaz' or long training. They did not need drugs to achieve the high level of creativity for which they became famous. One can be inventive through research. The genius does not need drugs to blossom. The hard worker can achieve excellence without resort to drugs by working hard over his identified area of creativity and talent. It could be an expression by composing a piece of art/sculpture/painting or by inventing a device. Creativity can be reflected through research and development. Every one of us can be creative in some or the other area. The need is to explore the area.

Physical Fitness

One has to be in good health and energetic to be able to feel enthusiastic. Exercises such as yoga, aerobics or jogging can be included in the daily routine. Where facilities exist, one should involve himself in outdoor activities like trekking, swimming, or playing outdoor games. Physical activities go a long way in keeping people away from the idle temptations like drugs or alcohol.

Positive Thinking

For emotional balance, there is nothing like positive thinking. The same situation can be viewed in more than one way. For the pessimist the glass is half empty while the positive thinker takes it as half full. There is the story of a salesman who was sent to Africa to sell shoes. He came back and reported, 'No one wears shoes in those countries, it is no use having a sales network'. Not satisfied with the report, the sales manager sent another salesman. He came back beaming and reported, 'No one has shoes in those countries, the scope is infinite'. The story shows how the whole attitude changes once things are perceived positively.

Positive thinking enhances one's capacity to manage one's moods and emotions. Cognitive restructuring can be learnt by sifting and analysing as has been discussed earlier. One way to help develop a positive attitude is to write all the thoughts that come across the mind. Sorting is the next step. This sorting must be done in the form of negative/positive thoughts. An analysis may lead to getting the ideas about how to make negative things positive. It is not surprising that one sad event leads one to remember a chain of sad events of life while it does not happen with happy moments. This chain reaction may be disrupted by consciously remembering the happy events that have occurred in life.

So much of happiness lies scattered around us. Sometimes just a feel of the cool breeze, the bright sunlight, murmuring of trees, silence of nature, sound of the flowing river, the glory of mountains can change the mood and enhance positive attitudes towards life. Occasional exposure to such natural settings can make one feel positive and grateful to the mercies that have been bestowed on all of us irrespective of our achievements or failures.

Some very small activities other than the daily routine can make us a changed person. One has only to try some of them. Dressing up differently, cooking or trying a new recipe or just playing with innocent children can be a very effective way of getting out of the drug net. Any of these could be tried, it will work as the best antiseptic against drug infection.

11

Drug Abuse Control

Practical Difficulties

Governments, all over the world, are conscious of the problems relating to drug abuse. The menace, however, has been spreading its tentacles to almost all geographical regions. The drug traffickers have been utilising very sophisticated techniques in their operations. The international control efforts find themselves almost outrun by the trafficking syndicates that operate at international levels. The traffickers are becoming ruthless and increasingly violent. The governments often find themselves beaten by the cartels that have established links with trade in illicit arms and subversive political groups.

According to Government spokesmen in India, the terrorists operating in Jammu and Kashmir comprise partly Afghan mercenaries. These are provided sophisticated arms obtained illegally and the whole operation is financed by money obtained from drug transit.

This is only one example where even a well-meaning government may find itself helpless in controlling the spread of drug menace. There are many more practical difficulties.

The first set of problems arises in the area of production. Poppy is grown in India both legally and illegally. The legal cultivation is covered under the provisions of the Narcotic Drugs and Psychotropic Substances Act. However, when it comes to implementation, corruption is a problem with which the Indian government cannot claim immunity. Illegal poppy is grown in areas which are not easily accessible. Often the cultivators enjoy political patronage. The growers can be very tough and cruel with the informers and the state is in no position to afford security against mafia tactics of the illegal growers. The profits from illicit sales leave enough margin for the people in business to corrupt enforcement officials and maintain their own toughs against any half-hearted efforts on the part of government agencies. While the democratic governments find themselves answerable for any damage that might be caused to the life of the illicit drug trafficker, the latter are bound by no such answerability. Human rights activists are unconcerned when enforcement officials are kidnapped or killed but deaths in encounters raise hue and cry at both – national and international-forums. This demoralises the state enforcement officials.

The problem of regulating the cultivation of drugs relating crops is further compounded by the fact that some crops just grow wild in the foothills e.g. *bhang*. Its leaves can be easily procured. One need not always go to the government licensed shop for its supply.

The second set of problem relates to the use of drugs by various social groups. *Bhang* in Hindu society has no stigma attached to it. As a matter of fact, its use is almost sanctified on certain religious festivals and occasions. Efforts to control its use make no sense as so often they run against popular beliefs. Offering opium to guests carries no taboo in certain societies in Rajasthan. Here also, any effort on the part of government or even NGOs comes across stiff resistance. Alcoholic drinks, most often brewed at home, are a compulsory item in a number of tribal functions. These habits are deeply ingrained in the communities. The tribal communities are so dispersed in habitation that the government agencies simply ignore them for reasons of difficulty in accessibility. Gateway drugs like tobacco present similar problems. It is near-impossible to keep communities out of this habit as tobacco chewing (in pan or as such) and smoking are part of social culture. As a matter of fact in a number of rural and backward communities the greatest punishment that the society inflicts on a defaulting member is to boycott him from smoking the hookah in the company of other members of the community. The fear of cancer notwithstanding, gateway drugs continue to have both social sanction and popularity across social and religious barriers. One religious community which is forbidden to smoke through a religious order is the Sikhs. But here again the restriction is often more than compensated by resort to alcohol.

Distribution through legal channels is also beset with a number of practical difficulties. Revenue considerations compel the state governments from enforcing any strict ban on the use of drugs. The excise levies push up the prices to a level where it becomes very lucrative to indulge in illicit trade even after the expenses on bribing the enforcement agencies and the risk of occasional raids has been taken care of. Alcoholic drinks, bhang, opium and many other drugs are sold through government licensed shops. There are built-in escape routes within the state laws. There is, for example, the provision for permits in case of addicts in case the open sale is banned. These loopholes are frequently exploited making a mockery of prohibition or state enforcement against use of drugs.

Curtailing the production of drug-producing crops has been tried in USA by introducing 'crop substitution programme' advising farmers to have alternative commercial crops. But it could not succeed for more than one reason. The substitute commercial crops cannot compete with drug-producing crops so far as the economic benefits are concerned. Moreover, the farmers do not have proper skills in producing alternative crops. Even if these problems are taken care of and production of drug producing crops curtailed, the addicts find substitutes for non-available drugs. The abuse of cough syrups or commonly prescribed medicines are such examples.

Sale of illicit drugs is now a well-managed industry that cuts across international frontiers. In cities like New Delhi there are 'joints' where smack becomes available to regular customers with so much ease as a packet of cigarettes. The kiosks near universities and colleges have regular customers and their own supply lines are heavily guarded yet very certain. These operate with the connivance of police and other not-so-honest enforcement officials.

It is an irony that the Excise Commissioner who organises the sale of liquor through auction of liquor vends in the State of Delhi is also the officer responsible for enforcing prohibition.

Of late, these drug traffickers have started involving influential politicians in their nefarious game. Trafficker-politician links are very difficult to tackle as the public officials are hesitant to take action against politicians who can always pull strings at the highest ministerial level and make things hot for honest officers. The control of drug abuse is becoming increasingly difficult with the growth of various uses to which drug earnings are now being used. Laundering black money is one such use (or abuse). Purchase of illicit arms is another. As already indicated financing mercenaries to fight proxy wars against a neighbouring country is the latest in the list.

Apart from naturally occurring drugs, synthetic drugs are now being added to the list. The latest is methaqualle, which is used as stimulant. It is a multi-billion trade which the governments have to check and control before the drugs put the entire progress of human civilisation into back gear destroying all that mankind has achieved through centuries of inventions and co-operation. The task is enormous but the consequences of failure are much too disastrous even to imagine.

There are many factors that cannot be countered through prevention programmes since they fall outside the limits of health education. They are problems of much bigger dimension and outside the scope of drug education or Tx. Sometimes these factors are economic. In societies where poverty is rampant or unemployment chronic, vulnerability to drug abuse becomes well beyond the effectiveness of the preventive measures. Similarly, where trafficking in drugs becomes a law and order problem, preventive measures lose their efficacy. Local campaigns against drug abuse are powerless against internationally organised mafias that have to be tackled at the international level. One Colombian drug lord – Carolos Lehder Rivas – said, "Cocaine is the Third World's atomic bomb". The way drug addiction is spreading into developed societies, this may not be an overstatement. Developing and least developed countries find it much easier to make money through drug channels than through normal trade. The laws are soft in their case and even when they are strict, the price for which violations can be secured is relatively less. While developed societies, as in USA, work hard to prevent entry of drugs in their country, underdeveloped societies produce drugs in large quantities notwithstanding international conventions.

Efforts to control flow of drugs in one country leads traffickers to search for new markets. For example, pressures from no-smoking lobby in USA is leading the manufacturers to open the markets in East. *Times of India* – June 19, 1994 reported, "The entry of western cigarette companies into Asia is expected to treble the annual worldwide death toll from tobacco-related illness to 10 million by the year 2050... the tobacco problem will dwarf tuberculosis and AIDS." The Tobacco Institute of India reportedly "looks forward to an 8-10 per cent growth in production and consumption of domestic tobacco." The new targets are going to be the yuppie, the liberated woman, the college students. The fact is noteworthy that government gives Rs. 28 crore for tobacco research and Rs. 1.4 crore for anti-tobacco education research !

Under sections 7 and 8 of the Environment Protection Act, 1986, non-smokers can prosecute a smoker for lighting up in front of them, and smokers can be punished with upto two years of imprisonment. While the law has never been taken seriously, last year, cigarette companies were banned from advertising in government sports stadia. In a number of cities, smoking is banned in government buildings.

Recently, the government has also called for a ban on cigarette advertising. In addition to the ban, the bill calls for a ban on tobacco sales within 100 metres of schools, hospitals, etc; a ban on smoking in public places, and more effective, prominently displayed, statutory warnings.

Does a ban on advertising make a difference ? Proponents and opponents of the ban tout conflicting figures. Advocates quote a 22-country study which found a lasting drop in countries which banned advertising. Panicky cigarette companies, in an eight-page advertising supplement, Tobacco : Myth and Reality, against the ban, argue that their sales have dropped even with advertising, while liquor sales have registered a steady climb, despite the ban on alcohol advertising.

Of course, they neglect to mention that liquor is actually advertised in disguise. And this is one problem with a ban – it is easily circumvented by advertising other products with the same name.

How does one ban a legal product? Especially after taxing it ? "This is one question that is regularly thrown back at me," says Ms Venkatesh. "I tell people *beedis* cause cancer, and they tell me, "How can the government let poisonous things be sold ? To that, I have no answer."

A ban may not be enforceable. But it is worth considering a ban on lifestyle advertising — selling cigarettes with scenes of people having fun — which is a powerful enticement to would-be smokers. In UK, the ban, along with the growing anti-smoking movement, has resulted in a sharp drop in smoking. There, advertisers must rely on pack shots instead of the Marlboro Man, puffing away as he communes with nature.

Unhygienic living conditions in developing countries make people cool towards slogans such as 'smoking causes cancer' or 'drugs lead to death'. Persons living on streets in scorching heat and rainy season, not getting even potable water to drink, hardly getting two meals a day and with no medical facilities for their health problems, do not bother about things that may happen after 10 years. For them the connection between a puff of 'smack' and death is too remote. These attitudes get promoted by the traffickers who are searching for markets at all costs. The advertising industries exploit this attitude to its fullest possibility.

Efforts at International Level

The responsibility for limiting the cultivation, production, manufacture and use of drugs to an adequate amount required for medicinal and scientific purposes rests with the International Narcotics Board with headquarters at Vienna. The convention of Narcotic Drugs, 1961 as amended by the 1972 Protocol makes the Board responsible for prevention of illicit cultivation, production and manufacture of and illicit traffic in and use of drugs. The Board functions in co-operation with governments and holds periodic consultation with the governments.

Besides the government, the Board also collaborates with United Nations Drug Control Programme. Its 13 members are drawn from different disciplines such as medicine and pharmacology. They serve in their personal capacity and not as representatives of their government. Other agencies with which the Board functions in co-operation are WHO and International Criminal Police Organisation. The Board prepares and publishes an annual report which contains an analysis of the drug control situation worldwide. Attention of the governments is drawn to gaps and weaknesses in national control and suggestions and recommendations are made for improvement at national and international levels.

The report of the International Narcotics Control Board for 1993 provides valuable information on the operation of the international drug control system besides analysis of the world situation.

In the overview for the last two decades, the Board's report for 1993 observed :

> "The economic power and political influence of drug cartels are rising. While drug abuse has been 'globalised', internationalisation and co-operation among drug cartels have also increased. There is also clear evidence that trafficking organisations barter different types of drugs among

> themselves. Drug trafficking syndicates are increasingly becoming involved in other forms of organised and violent crime, making use of sophisticated technical aids and modern communication systems. Criminal organisations control drugs from the cultivation and production phases to the storage and distribution phases. Large amounts of drugs are stored at staging posts in certain countries to take advantage of weak or ineffective laws in those countries. There is evidence that drug trafficking organisations frequently make use of the territories of countries (*a*) that are not parties to the international drug control treaties; (*b*) that have formally ratified conventions without implementing their provisions; (*c*) that suffer from civil war, terrorist activities; political instability, ethnic conflict, economic depression or social tension; (*d*) that are not in a position to ensure governmental control over some parts of their territories; and (*e*) that are not able to maintain adequate law enforcement, customs and pharmaceutical control services."

The United Nations Convention against Illicit Traffic in Narcotic Drugs and Psychotropic Substances, 1988 created a global mechanism against international drug-related activities. More and more countries are becoming party to the 1988 convention. Some of the countries in South America have been the main targets of criminal organisations. These countries are now taking initiative for adoption of 1988 convention. This is a healthy and encouraging development.

The report adds :

> "In 1993, Governments have demonstrated again that the closest international co-operation possible is required to fight the worldwide scourge of drug abuse and illicit trafficking. The Government Assembly, therefore, convened five high-level plenary sessions to examine the status of such international co-operation. Its adoption in October 1993, of resolution 48/12, on measures to strengthen international co-operation against the illicit production, sale, demand, traffic and distribution of narcotic drugs and psychotropic substances and related activities, may prove to be a significant step towards the further development of a common strategy and international machinery against drug abuse and illicit traffic. General Assembly resolution 48/12 is a clear

> manifestation of the determination of Governments to increase their co-operation with international organisations and each other in the fight against drug problems, which threaten the basic fabric of society and the political stability of nations."

The efforts of the Board are, however, handicapped by deficiencies in Government's compliance so far as reporting obligations are concerned. Yet another matter of concern as voiced by the Board in its report has been stated in the following words :

> "The Board is deeply concerned that, more than 20 years after the adoption of the 1971 Convention, some of the major manufacturing and exporting countries have not yet become parties to it and have not introduced control measures for international trade in many psychotropic substances. This situation is undermining the functioning of the international control system for psychotropic substances and has had a particularly negative impact on numerous developing countries where the abuse of those substances is prevalent."

Apart from drugs,

> "There is striking evidence that the abuse of stimulants is increasing in all regions of the world. Substantial quantities of fenetylline tablets have been seized in West Asia; the smuggling of amphetamine and pemoline into Africa has continued; the regular abuse of amphetamine tablets by bus drivers has been reported in south-east Asia; amphetamine is the main drug of abuse in Scandinavian countries and in some other European countries; the abuse of methyl-enedioxymethamphetamine (MDMA), commonly known as "ecstasy" has been the cause of many night-time road accidents in Europe; many clandestine methamphetamine laboratories have been dismantled in North America and in east Asia; as the abuse of ephedrine (methcathinone) constitutes a major drug problem in the Commonwealth of Independent States (CIS) and the same compound is synthesised in clandestine laboratories in North America. Increasing quantities of khat (catha edulis) are being exported from producer countries to Australia and to countries in Europe and North America. The Board invites

> Governments to co-operate in preventing large-scale illicit trafficking in stimulants and to study the extent and pattern of the abuse of those substances listed in the 1971 Convention or other substances not subject to international control, such as ephedrine or khat."

On the importance of demand reduction, the Board has highlighted the view that the solution of drug problem lies simply in suppressing illicit production in supplier countries and reducing demand in consumer countries is just not valid. The classification of countries as suppliers, consumers or just transit countries is just not valid today as it never was. All the same it is important that drug supply is controlled for without that drug consumption can never be successfully attained. "If drugs are readily available and easily accessible, new drug abusers will soon replace the former ones."

It is evident that, at the national level, supply reduction and demand reduction cannot be separated from each other. There is, however, a major difference at the international level. Measures against the illicit manufacture, production, traffic and diversion of drugs can be 'codified' in international treaties, because their identical application constitutes the *sine qua non* criteria for the functioning of the international drug control system. Demand reduction methods, however, cannot be 'standardised' by legal documents.

The first and foremost important step in any drug control programme is demand reduction. The importance of demand reduction was initially realised by the international community 20 years ago: the idea was translated into the provisions of the 1971 Convention, followed immediately by the amendment of the 1961 Convention by the 1972 Protocol. It is noteworthy that the 1988 Convention, which was intended to be a convention explicitly against illicit traffic, also contains provisions for demand reduction.

While demand reduction has to be the first priority of the Governments, prevention or at least reduction of illicit supply of drugs is no less important. It is also noteworthy that the international efforts to control of drugs should not create a shift from drugs to alcohol or other organic substances which at the national level are most available without restriction.

> "Thus, it is of the utmost importance that reduction of the demand for all substances of abuse be the goal of such

> national programmes. That philosophy is reflected in the WHO approach to the problem : the WHO Programme on Substance Abuse is comprehensive and not limited to narcotic drugs and psychotropic substances. The Board commends the WHO Expert Committee on Drug Dependence for drawing renewed attention to the problems associated with the use of tobacco, alcohol and other drugs in its recently published twenty-eighth report. The Board welcomes the emphasis placed by the Expert Committee on the need for a comprehensive approach in combating the abuse of psychoactive drugs. The Board notes that such a comprehensive approach is also present in the UNESCO preventive education strategy."

The problem of reduction in drug demand is beset with a number of social constraints that operate in individual societies. As discussed earlier, in India, for example, drugs or *bhang* (cannabis) are associated with a number of pseudo-religious practices among a section of the Hindus. Demand reduction strategies have, therefore, to be designed keeping in view not only the individuals but also the socio-cultural economic milieu in which they operate.

> Community empowerment in relation to drug abuse is often the key link between education and treatment services. Its purpose is to promote the extent to which a community feels that it has some control over the process of making decisions that directly affect them. Especially in circumstances where there may be a virtual absence of social controls, this approach can be crucial to the success of both demand and supply reduction strategies. Strengthening the cohesiveness of communities is, therefore, one of the most important tasks.

Education programmes must be carefully designed in order to avoid being counter-productive. Support may be given to mass media campaigns to raise public awareness concerning the dangers of drug abuse. The principal target group for education programmes are young people, both in and out of school. Programmes for the promotion of a healthy lifestyle that incorporate a drug prevention element should be encouraged. It must be kept in mind that in many developing countries with inadequate health-and social-care services, education programmes are practically the only medium available for demand reduction activities.

The success of demand reduction programmes depends on two factors – the political will of Governments to tackle the problem, as evidenced by, among other things, the provision of the necessary financial resources; and the community's willingness to co-operate. Without following 'top-down' and 'bottom-up' approaches simultaneously, it is not realistic to expect positive results from demand reduction programmes.

The Board, in its report for 1993, has noted with satisfaction the encouraging results obtained by community-based approaches in countries like India, Myanmar and Sri Lanka. It notes with particular emphasis that in Myanmar, such an approach led to a considerable reduction in drug-related crimes.

> "Successful demand reduction projects have also been reported by UNDCP. An integrated demand reduction project in Pakistan has succeeded in raising awareness among students and the general public concerning the dangers of drug abuse. Intervention teams involving a number of non-governmental organisations have directed community services in public education, community organisation and treatment services for the prevention and reduction of drug problems. In Colombia, municipal authorities at Bogota have been successfully involved in the implementation of a project for the prevention of drug abuse. The project, which is aimed at reducing risk factors leading to drug abuse, has focused on the individual, the family and the community. In Bolivia, targetting a well-defined group – in this case, street children – has been regarded as the reason for the good results achieved by a project for the development of strategies and policies to protect street children by promoting an alternative lifestyle through education, training, counselling and the creation of alternative employment possibilities."

> Many States have made effective changes to laws and regulations; have become parties to the 1988 Convention; have adopted most or all of the recommendations on strengthening the efforts of the international community in the fight against money-laundering, adopted by the Financial

Action Task Force established by the heads of State or Government of the Group of Seven major industrialised countries and the President of CEC; have complied with the Council of the European Communities directive 91/308/EEC of 10 June, 1991 on prevention of the use of the financial system for the purpose of money-laundering; or have adopted model regulations concerning laundering offences connected to illicit drug trafficking and related offences, adopted in 1992 by the Inter-American Drug Abuse Control Commission (CICAD) of the Organization of American States (OAS). Coordination of the international efforts against money-laundering is intended to lead ultimately to effective programmes within most countries, thereby ensuring that effective legislation is implemented, investigations are conducted, practical measures are taken within the financial system, cross-border currency flow and suspicious currency transactions are reported and international cooperation is enhanced through the use of treaties of mutual legal assistance.

Money-laundering countries, however, mainly as a result of the increasing sophistication and changing tactics of drug traffickers get past to launder their proceeds. Daring traffickers seek countries and territories with weak central banks, restrictive bank secrecy practices and limited controls on foreign exchange. Experience indicates that even where jurisdictions have enacted laws making money-laundering a criminal offence, such laws are likely to be ineffective unless bank, corporate and official secrecy requirements are relaxed, subject to appropriate safeguards. The 1988 Convention calls for relaxation of bank secrecy requirements in cases involving drug trafficking, including drug-related money-laundering. Complementary provisions are often required to limit opportunities for money-laundering and to ensure that if it occurs, documents and money can be traced to the satisfaction of the courts.

While the international community has been striving to reduce availability and access to drugs, instances are not wanting where the governments have legalisation of drug abuse. In 1993, Italy issued a decree repealing the prohibition of the non-medical use of drugs.

Such measures necessarily make more drugs easily available and are counter to drug-abuse efforts. Some other countries where INCB sent missions to review the functioning of drug control systems include Bolivia, Bulgaria, Colombia, Costa Rica, Denmark, India, Israel, Kenya, Myanmar, Nicaragua, Peru, Poland, South Africa, Uruguay and Zambia. It is hoped that the visit of the mission will be followed up with positive steps by the concerned governments to implement the recommendations with respect to functioning of drug control systems.

How the International Drug Control System Operates

A total of 144 States were parties to the international convention on narcotic drugs. However, as many as 14 States in Africa, six in Asia, five in Caribbean and five in South Pacific have yet to become parties to the international convention on narcotic drugs. Many CIS member-States and newly independent States in eastern Europe have yet to indicate whether they intend to succeed or accede to the international convention on narcotic drugs.

The diversion of narcotic drugs into illicit traffic can be effectively checked only if the necessary information asked for by the INCB is regularly supplied by the States. The position in this respect is far from satisfactory.

> "In respect of the statistical data required under Article 20 of the 1961 Convention, 115 States and territories submitted complete statistical information for 1992. A total of 48 States, including China, Luxembourg, Morocco, New Zealand and Pakistan, have so far furnished only partial data for 1992. No statistical data for 1992 have been received from 24 States and territories : Afghanistan, Antigua and Barbuda, Bermuda, Bolivia, Cambodia, Cameroon, Djibouti, Gabon, Ghana, Gibraltar, Grenada, Kenya, Liberia, Mauritania, Papua New Guinea, Saint Lucia, Solomon Islands, Somalia, Sudan, Tristan da Cunha, Turks and Caicos Islands, United Republic of Tanzania, Vietnam and Zambia. Some of those States and territories have failed to furnish statistical data for several consecutive years.

The Board notes with satisfaction that Azerbaijan, Croatia, Estonia, Kyrgyzstan, Latvia, Lithuania and Republic of Moldova have begun to apply the provisions of the 1961 Convention by furnishing their own estimates and statistical data. The Board has been informed that the Standing Committee on Narcotic Drugs Control of the Russian Federation will, for the time being, fulfil certain obligations of the international drug control treaties on behalf of Georgia and the following CIS member-States : Armenia, Belarus, Kazakhstan, Kyrgyzstan, Republic of Moldova, Russian Federation, Tajikistan, Turkmenistan, Ukraine and Uzbekistan."

A very peculiar situation has arisen as a result of many organisations having become involved in providing humanitarian assistance because of war or political instability in several regions. That assistance has in some cases included narcotic drugs. The narcotic drugs, thus provided, have been diverted to illicit channels by the recipient countries.

There are some genuine difficulties involved in conducting international trade in narcotic drugs *vis-a-vis* the need for urgent supply of essential narcotic drugs to war-torn countries. If the import-export authorisation is made easy, there is the danger of the drugs finding their way to street markets. In case the authorisations are made strict that may hamper quick availability of narcotic drugs needed in humanitarian situations. An initiative has since been taken by the government of Denmark by way of establishing a supply division in co-operation with UNICEF to facilitate the supply of narcotic drugs and psychotropic substances by UNICEF and the full implementation of the provisions of the international drug control treaties.

Codeine Preparations Abuse

Codeine is largely used in cough syrups. In a number of countries, codeine preparations are sold without a medical prescription. INCB has, in its report, desired that the concerned countries should take measures to ensure that codeine is not abused as drug.

Zipeprol Abuse

Zipeprol is presently out of international control. The substance is being used in France and Italy for opiate like effects. In Brazil there have been more than 50 reported deaths as a result of overdose of zipeprol. The drug is also available in a number of South American countries. The INCB is seriously considering the case for possible scheduling of zipeprol under international drug control treaties.

Heroin Abuse

"Following a decision of the Government of Switzerland to conduct a scientific research project involving the prescription of heroin to drug abusers during treatment, it was brought to the attention of the Board that, in Germany, the city of Frankfurt had applied to the Federal Health Office for permission to conduct a similar scientific research project. Moreover, the German Bundesrat (federal council), which represents the 16 Lander (provinces), had introduced a bill for consideration by the Bundestag (parliament) under which heroin and other narcotic drugs that had been neither marketed nor available on prescription could be used for research purposes. The Board has taken note that the Government of Germany rejected the bill and that the application submitted by the city of Frankfurt will not be granted. The Board welcomes the decisions reached in Germany and hopes that similar situations in other countries will be resolved in the same manner. As in the report of the Board for 1992, Governments are reminded that resolutions of the Economic and Social Council and the Commission on Narcotic Drugs, as well as recommendations of WHO, call for the prohibition of heroin manufacture, export, import, and use on human beings."

Production of Opiate Raw Materials and its Consumption

"The increase in global production of opiate raw materials in 1991 and 1992 had an adverse effect on the balance between global production of opiate raw materials and total consumption of opiates. In 1993, however, global production of opiate raw materials was below total consumption by only about seven tonnes in morphine equivalent. According to forecasts, the balance between total production of opiate raw material and global consumption of opiates is likely to be restored in 1994. In view of the need to maintain a lasting balance between demand for and supply of opiates, the Board once again urges the Governments concerned to restrict global production of opiate raw materials to a level corresponding to actual needs in opiates and to refrain from any proliferation of production.

Export and Import of Opiate Raw Materials

In India, opium exports fell to 55 tonnes in morphine equivalent in 1992, following two successive years in which more than 60 tonnes of morphine equivalent were exported annually. The 1992 decline appears to have been caused not only by a lack of imports by CIS member-States in that year, but also by significant reductions in the quantities imported by the United Kingdom of Great Britain and Northern Ireland, the United States of America and, above all, France. Of the main opium importers, only Japan increased its imports in 1992, to nearly 11 tonnes in morphine equivalent. In absolute terms, the United States remained the largest opium importer in 1992, having imported 36 tonnes in morphine equivalent; France and the United Kingdom, other main importers, imported 0.2 tonne and 7.2 tonnes in morphine equivalent, respectively. By contrast, exports of concentrate of poppy straw, which had declined to 64 tonnes in morphine equivalent in 1990 and 1991 following a peak of 88 tonnes in morphine equivalent in 1988, rose to 69 tonnes in morphine equivalent in 1992. Australia has steadily increased its share of exports of poppy straw. Other main exporters of concentrate of poppy straw in 1992 were Hungry, Turkey, France and Spain, in that order. In 1992, the United Kingdom imported a record quantity of 35 tonnes of concentrate of poppy straw in morphine equivalent, principally from Australia, while the Netherlands imported 12 tonnes in morphine equivalent and the United States imported from Australia, France and Turkey a total of 8.5 tonnes in morphine equivalent. At informal consultations organised by the Board in response to Council resolutions 1992/30 and 1993/37, the representatives of countries that are major importers of opium raw materials reaffirmed the intention of their Governments to maintain the current policy of according priority to importing opiate raw materials from traditional supplier countries."

Psychotropic Substances

There are at present 126 countries that are party to the 1971 Convention. However, a number of States do not regularly provide information pursuant to Article 16 of the 1971 Convention. That makes the task of identifying companies or individuals violating national legislation or attempting to divert such substances into illicit channels difficult. Yet another problem is that a number of States such as Australia, Belgium and Switzerland have not yet adopted legislation necessary for effective control of all psychotropic substances. These States are major producers and exporters of psychotropic substances.

Cases are known where psychotropic substances were manufactured with the intention of exporting them into illicit channels. In 1993, the Government of India investigated the case of more than 30 commercial orders. The orders involved millions of tablets containing pemoline, chlordiazepoxide, diazepam, phenobarbital and buprenorphine. These tablets are normally used as stimulants, tranquillizers, analgesics and anti-epleptics in licit channels. The tablets were destined for export to countries in Africa, Central America and eastern Europe. The Narcotics Commissioner of India conducted the investigations in collaboration with INCB.

Illicit trafficking in psychotropic drugs is also carried on through diversions where the control systems are relatively weak. In one case it was found that pemoline tablets manufactured in Asia were first exported to Luxembourg and then reexported to Nigeria with the support of a trading company located in United Kingdom. It is noteworthy that import of pemoline had been prohibited in Nigeria.

The control of illicit trade in psychotropic substances is rather difficult in countries where parallel medical systems operate. In India, for example, there are ayurvedic drugs that are outside the control of the drug legislations. Often these preparations (Sura for example) contain heavy doses of alcohol or other substances that are psychotropic in effort.

The INCB's observations in this respect are :

> "The Board has observed that many Governments particularly in Africa and South America, have, in their national health and drug control policies, not yet given adequate attention to the control of distribution channels for pharmaceutical products. In many of those countries, the existence of "parallel" distribution systems, in combination with the widespread practice of self-medication, has led to, *inter alia,* uncontrolled use of psychotropic substances. The long-term public health consequences of that development have not yet been fully assessed. The Board wishes to call the attention of all the Governments concerned to this issue and reiterates the need for a balanced drug control policy that ensures the provision of the necessary resources to drug regulatory authorities. Furthermore, in some countries that have adequate legislation on the control of distribution channels,

the implementation of the legislation is hampered by the lack of administrative arrangements regarding coordination and cooperation between drug regulatory authorities and law enforcement authorities, including both customs and police. The Board invites international bodies such as UNDCP and WHO to support Governments in their efforts to adequately control distribution channels for pharmaceutical products."

Control of Solvents

A number of chemicals are used in the manufacture of substances like cocaine or heroin. Acetic anhydride is used to convert morphine to heroin. In many cases exports from chemical producing countries are of a suspicious nature. In the case of Latin America it was found that there has been an increase in cultivation of poppy. This was compounded by increased imports of shipments of solvents used in the manufacture of narcotic drugs in illicit trade. The seizure of shipments of chemical substances reflects intensified efforts by States, yet the fact remains that such seizures reflect only a small fraction of the total illicit trade.

Substances frequently used in the illicit manufacture of narcotic drugs or psychotropic substances are referred to as precursors. The need for further action by governments in control of precursors has been emphasised by the INCB.

In general, despite a number of recent initiatives there is still a need for greater awareness of the importance of establishing effective control over precursors with all control authorities and with the chemical industry. Within geographical regions, in particular, control measures should be harmonised so that weak controls in one country do not jeopardise the efforts of neighbouring countries, where controls may be more effective. Otherwise, it will seriously limit the effectiveness of regional and global efforts to prevent diversion of such substances, since weak links at the domestic level will be exploited by those involved in illicit drug manufacture. The Board calls upon all Governments to exercise the greatest vigilance in identifying suspicious transactions and to take all necessary steps to prevent the diversion of precursors to illicit traffic.

The term precursor is used to indicate any of the substances in Table I or II of the 1988 Convention, except where the context requires a different expression. Such substances are often described as precursors or essential chemicals, depending on their principal chemical properties. The plenipotentiary conference that adopted the Convention did not use any one term to describe such substances. Instead, the expression "substances frequently used in the illicit manufacture of narcotic drugs or psychotropic substances" was introduced in the Convention. It has become common practice, however, to refer to all such substances simply as precursors; although that term is not technically correct.

In order for arrangements of this type to work, importing countries need to identify the competent authorities and their roles in controlling imports and communicate this information to exporting countries. There should also be an appropriate mechanism by which such authorities can respond promptly to inquiries from exporting countries. Without such efforts by the importing countries, pre-export notifications and export authorisations cannot prevent diversion.

In addition to monitoring international trade, for which Article 12 of the 1988 Convention stipulates mandatory measures, Governments should pay equal attention, where applicable, to controlling domestic manufacture and distribution of precursors. There is information indicating that chemicals necessary for the illicit manufacture of heroin, and also of cocaine, are often smuggled through borders into countries where illicit drug manufacture is taking place. The problem has many dimensions, while efforts continue at international level to combat the menace. Nations must also come forward to make their territories drug-free zones.

India has drawn a National Master Plan for Drug Abuse Control spread over the years 1994-2000. Some of the important facets of the drug menace which have been identified as needing urgent attention are inadequate facilities for treatement of addicts, specially those from low income groups living in urban slums, illegal cultivation of cannabis and opium, rapid growth in manufacturing facilities for heroin and mandrax and the increasing use of long unmanned India coast line for smuggling. The plan candidly admits that counter-measures have not increased correspondingly.

The Narcotic Drugs and Psychotropic Substances (NDPS) Act nets only small fish. In January 1993, it was found that nearly two-thirds of the cases sent for trial were still pending decision. Even in the cases decided, the rate of conviction was as low as 10.3 per cent.

It is obvious that the law has little or no deterrent effect. The plan calls for a national drug abuse control programme to combat the drug menace. It also proposes a National Control Board for Narcotics and Psychotropic Substances to monitor new substances entering the market.

The ideal still remains a distant dream. It is time mankind took up the challenge since even nature cannot help species from extinction unless it is willing to heed the signals and adapt to emerging situations.

12

Drug-Related Behaviours

(A Case Study – Delhi University)

The study is based on a sample of 350 students of Delhi University and affiliated colleges who were frequent users of alcohol and other drugs. Some of them were addicts. The students visited the Aptitude Testing Centre attached to Delhi University for help from the author who had been there as the Psychologist. Most students did not in the first instance disclose that they wanted help to get over their drug-related problems. They projected their need for aptitude testing, career guidance and counselling as these services were available at the Centre.

It was during the counselling/therapy sessions that it came out that students were frequent users of drugs.

The sample under study includes both male and female students. The analysis given in the study is based on information provided on Background Data Forms, personality test scores, interviews and counselling sessions. The students covered in the study were from the arts/science/professional streams as well as Ph.D. students. Some of the students also came from medical colleges/IIT and other professional institutes. Students came to the Centre voluntarily and also along with their friends or boy/girl friends. Very few cases were referred to by the parents.

No highly sophisticated statistical techniques were used in the study as the primary purpose was to have an idea of the total dimension of the problem and to provide them guidance that would enable them to lead a drug-free normal life. It was considered desirable by the author that there should be no formal structuring of the information through questionnaires or the like except personal/family data since that would inhibit the natural flow of information that was coming through an atmosphere of trust and understanding between the students and the Psychologist Counsellor.

The hard core addicts were referred to the appropriate de-addiction centres. Their cases are not included in the study. The results of the study have been given in the following tables. Percentages have been rounded off to nearest whole number.

Sex Distribution

The sex-wise distribution of the drug abusers is shown in table 12.1.

Table 12.1

Sex	Percentage
Male	78
Female	22
Total	**100**

Out of the students who came for help and are included in the study, 78 per cent comprise males and 22 per cent females. The figure 22 per cent shows that the conventional image of girls being severely inhibited is not borne out by facts emerging from the study.

Types of Drugs Abused

Information was collected with respect to the various drugs abused by the students frequently. The following table illustrates the percentage distribution over different drugs.

Table 12.2
Percentage Distribution over Different Drugs

Drugs	Percentage of abusers
Cigarette / Tobacco	68
Alcohol	82
Sleeping/Waking pills	22
Anti-depressants	29
Cannabis	42
Heroin	07
LSD	01
* Others	03

* (*Many students took more than one drug. Hence, the total does not come to 100.*)

Smoking and alcohol were found to be the most commonly used drugs among the students. Girls were no exception to the use of cigarettes or alcohol. During interviews, it was found that the girls would rather take alcohol than smoke in the company of their boy friends and other friends not necessarily girls. Boys had no such inhibitions. They would take drugs and alcohol or cigarettes with their girl friends or other exclusive male groups.

Waking pills were common among the girls during the examination days. Sleeping pills and other depressants were taken to cope with stress and tensions and even to get a good nap.

Girls took tobacco in the form of cigarettes only. Boys smoked cigarettes and also chewed tobacco with lime. Hard drinks and drugs were not common with girl students.

Many students including girls took more than one drug. Smoking and drinking often went together in the case of girls. The boys combined cigarettes, alcohol and hard drugs. Smoking and alcohol were also popular with a large number of students who did not come to the Centre. This was revealed by the clients and confirmed by almost every one attending the centre.

Drug Initiation

Friends were the most common initiators. The students, however, insisted that the decision to smoke, drink or take drugs was their own. There was no compulsion from the friends offering beer or a cigarette. There were some hesitations and inhibitions in the first instance but these were soon overcome as everybody else was taking them. Some students hailing from the states of Uttar Pradesh and Bihar admitted that they were pressurised to take cigarettes or alcohol. The following table shows the role of initiators.

Table 12.3
Role of Initiators

Initiators	Percentage
Friends	61
Self	19
Relatives	11
Foreigners/Strangers	06
Others	03
Total	**100**

The relatives as initiators were mostly cousins who were used to smoking or drinking. Foreigners living in the hostels also influenced and acted as initiators in case of a number of students residing in hostels.

Of the 19 per cent students who had initiated themselves to drugs, most started off with anti-depressants taken as medicines. The category included neighbours who acted as initiators in some cases. The strange cases were of those students who came from families where taking alcohol was an accepted norm at festive and religious ceremonies. In such cases the initiators include father and in some cases even the mother.

Place of Initiation

The following table shows the distribution over various places of initiation.

Table 12.4
Place of Drug Initiation

Places	Percentage
Parties	57
Hostel	24
Friend's house	07
College campus	04
Home	02
Others	06
Total	**100**

The table shows that parties were the most vulnerable place where college students were introduced to drugs in the first instance. Students found it difficult and embarrassing to say 'no' on such occasions. Hostels were other common places where casualties occurred. Initiation of drugs at home was very low as there was the inherent fear of being caught. College campus was also low in the list. Other places included the pan shop, tea stall or a neighbour's house.

Source of Supply

Students were asked about the source of their supply. The supply points and their distribution is shown in the following table:

Table 12.5
Percentage Distribution over Supply Points

Supply points	Percentage
Friends	38
Pushers/Peddlers	22
Pan shops	13
Foreigners	11
College kiosks	07
Medical stores	05
Others	04
Total	**100**

The table shows that friends were a continuous source of drug supply. Pushers and peddlers came next. Students who got initiated knew from where they could have their next dose. Pan shops and college kiosks were regular and frequent suppliers even within the campus. Students revealed that it was very easy to get alcohol in soft drink bottles at the college kiosks and other shops. 'Other' supply points included relations, neighbours etc.

Funding Expenditure on Drugs

Table 12.6
Source for Drug Funding

Income Source	Percentage
Pocket money	42
Loans from friends	29
Loans from others	08
Theft	04
Sale of personal effects	05
Earnings from drug pushing	08
Any other	04
Total	**100**

The table clearly demonstrates that pocket money was the most frequent source for procuring drugs. Large number of students borrowed money from friends. In some cases the students had sold off their books or personal belongings to get money. Drug peddlers often used the abusers for pushing drugs among friends and paid cash or drug itself by way of commission.

It was found that funding for drugs was rarely from a single source. Sometimes it was stealing from the house, another time it was borrowing and so on. Other sources included loans from relations feigning sickness, family need or some other lie. Where money was not available to satisfy the craving, the abusers in many cases did not hesitate to steal household effects and sell them at throwaway prices.

Reasons for Taking Drugs

The students gave wide variety of reasons as to why they took recourse to drugs. The following table shows the frequency distribution over the variety of causes.

Table 12.7
Reasons for Drug Intake

Reasons for resorting to drugs	Percentage
Peer pressure	41
Symbol of modernity	28
Curiosity	21
Craving for excitement	17
Depression	09
Coping with stress	07
Boosting sex behaviours	06
Idle time	05
Family discords	04
Rebel against authority	04
Failure in love	03
Prelude to creative efforts	01
* Any other	03

It is evident from the table that peer pressure was the most important causative factor followed by drugs as a symbol of modernity. Sheer curiosity came next in the list. It also emerged during the discussion that the students resorted to drugs for more than one reason. Peer pressure often combined with curiosity while depression was so often a fall-out of failure in love etc. *(*This explains why the total percentage accounted for by different causes is more than 100.*)

One thing that stands out from this study and analysis of the available data is that college-going age is the most vulnerable so far as drug temptations are concerned. Friends and peers influence drug-related behaviours. From the earlier tables it is evident that a high percentage of students is initiated into taking drugs due to peer pressure. It seems that curiosity is there and a little motivation from friends leads newcomers to overcome the initial inhibitions and submission to drugs as the symbol of modernity and free living.

Residential Status of Students

In the study, attempt was also made to find out as to who were more prone to drug abuse — the day scholars or the hostelers. The results are reflected in the following table.

Table 12.8
Residential Status of Drug Abusers

Residential Status	Percentage
Hostelers	68
Day scholars	21
Lodgers in private premises	09
Others	02
Total	**100**

Hostelers formed the most prone group. Further probing revealed that day scholars were afraid of being detected due to direct supervision by parents at home. Such control was absent in the case of hostelers and hence the much larger incidence. The higher percentage in case of hostelers was also explained by the fact that they were exposed to peer pressure for much longer durations. Participation in group parties was less frequent in the case of day scholars. Lodgers in private premises or with relations were afraid of being thrown out once their abuse of drugs was detected. This fear acted as their shield against drug abuse.

Sex-Related Behaviours of Male Drug Abusers

Table 12.9
Sex Indulgence

Sex Partner	Percentage
Professional prostitutes	31
Callgirls	15
Girl friends	11
College mates	06
Others	03
Not disclosed	22
Not indulged	12
Total	**100**

It was alarming to note that high percentage of drug abusers sought sex gratifications in professional prostitutes. The richer and elite students preferred callgirls. Students were very keen to project a clean image among their girl friends and classmates and as such chose professionals rather than having sex with their own classmates or college friends. Sex with collegemates or girl friends was in most of the cases was confined to cases where both the partners were drug abusers.

Visiting professionals for sex gratification by abuser males were not found to be a regular phenomenon. There were cases of just one or two visits sometimes for curiosity sake. Some students also disclosed that in many cases the students had never dared to climb the steps of professional prostitutes but bragged about it simply as a daring male behaviour. It would not be fair to draw any statistically accurate conclusions under the circumstances except that sex sanctity among the student community is no longer as respected as it was many years ago.

Perception of being Drug Abuser

Table 12.10
Perception towards Drug Abuse

Perception	Percentage
No	87
Yes	5
Cannot say	8
Total	**100**

Eighty-seven per cent of the drug abusers stated that they did not regard themselves as abusers or addicts. Drugs, according to them, were something that most people took and, therefore, a way of life rather than an aberration. Alcohol and cigarettes were not regarded as drugs even by frequent smokers and those taking alcohol. The drug abusers maintained that since they did not take drugs regularly, they were not addicts. Only 5 per cent were willing to take upon themselves the label of being addicts. Other 8 per cent were not sure about their status although they frequently used drugs.

Feelings about Drug Abuse

Did they suffer a feeling of guilt while using drugs ? The findings are reflected below :

Table 12.11
Feelings about taking Drugs

Feelings	Percentage
Feel high	62
Ashamed	11
Felt guilty	21
Any other	06
Total	**100**

Far from being ashamed or feeling guilty, 62 per cent students felt high about their abusing drugs. Mere 11 per cent felt ashamed. Six per cent students were not able to analyse their feelings. However, they wanted that their parents must not know about their drug abuse.

The great majority felt that drug abuse made them feel acceptable in their group.

The reason why most students did not have a feeling of guilt or shame could also be explained by the fact that the students did not regard themselves as addicts or abusers. So the question of feeling guilty did not arise.

The whole analysis is based on unstructured interviews and information given by the students in strict confidence. Where possible the emerging trends have been confirmed from other sources also. All the same they are indicative of radically changing attitudinal structure so far as the abuse of drugs among students is concerned.

Whether Drug Abuse is in Parental Knowledge :

Table 12.12
Drug Abuse and Parental Knowledge

Parental Knowledge	Percentage
Yes	37
No	52
Don't know	11
Total	**100**

The table shows that over half of the parents of the drug abusers were unaware about the status of their wards. Even in the case of 37 per cent parents who knew about the indulgence of their wards, their knowledge was restricted to their wards smoking or taking alcohol occasionally. They had no idea that their wards even took recourse to hard drugs. Permissiveness on the part of parents is rather a recent phenomenon. These parental attitudes need a different study.

Drug Abuse by Parents

Table 12.13
Parental Drug Abuse

Parents	Percentage
Father	92
Mother	37

It was found that in the case of drug abusers, as many as 92 per cent had fathers who were taking alcohol. Mothers constitute 37 per cent although the figures relate only to casual drinking. These percentages in part explain permissiveness on the part of the parents.

The drugs used by the parents included sleeping pills besides alcoholic drinks. Other drugs in vogue were cigarettes and anti-depressants. Young boys and girls in many cases took part in parties held at home where they took alcoholic drinks in the presence of their parents. In the case of mothers, cigarette smoking was most confined to women groups where 'kitty parties' were frequent.

Exercise of Parental Control

The drug abusers were asked whether their parents ever felt concerned about their late arrivals at home, the way they used their pocket money or the choice of friends. These were regarded as indexes of parental control. The results were as follows :

Table 12.14
Parental Control

Parents exercise control	34%
Do not exercise control	66%
Total	**100**

Even in the case of 34 per cent, it was found that parental control was minimal and not as restrictive as when the boys or girls were at school. There was some severity in enforcing home reporting time in the evenings in respect of girls. Families higher up in economic status exercised fewer controls in matters relating to their wards studying in colleges and universities.

Career Planning

Drug abusers were asked about their future career plans and the responses given by them are reflected in the following table.

Table 12.15
Drug Abuse in relation to Career Planning

Whether Specific Career Plans existed	Percentage
Yes	23
No	77
Total	**100**

Great majority of the 23 per cent with specific career plans belonged to professional courses and the Ph.D. scholars. Most of them with no specific career plans belonged to humanities streams or other Hons. courses. Either way it indicates that students who had clear career motivations were less likely to be tempted than those without any specific career plans.

Leisure Time Planning

The following table shows how the students included in the study spent their leisure time. It has already been discussed elsewhere in the book that there is plenty of leisure time available with college and university students in India and for which no organised activities exist.

Table 12.16
Leisure Time Pursuits

Leisure Time Activity	Percentage
Visiting friends	48
Watching T.V.	38
Listening to music	29
Watching movies	27
Playing games	12
Reading books	06
Social service	01
* Others	08

** (Since most students took part in more than one activity the total exceeds 100)*

The picture that emerges from the statistics given above is that a very large number of students have no planned activities for creative use of their leisure time. Visiting friends is just another name for 'peer-pressure'. Similarly watching T.V. or listening to music is another passive activity very popular with them. Western culture-oriented programmes were found popular among those who were interested in watching T.V. and disco/western music was more popular than Indian music. Those who could afford went to discos or organised parties. In many cases parents felt elated at the idea that their children too went to parties knowing very well what goes on in these late-night sessions.

Discussion of Results

The findings of the study are alarming since they relate to that group of the society over which so much money is being invested by the public exchequer by way of highly subsidised college education. The society is entitled to a fair return on its investments fr. .ı these university trained boys and girls. But if they choose the dark alleys of drug abuse, far from repaying the investment, more money would be needed to de-addict and support rehabilitation programmes. This is unfair on the tax-payers and also on the priority sectors whose demands are cut down for want of enough state funds. It is reiterated that the study does not relate to hard addicts. It is also not the case of the investigator that all those who are one-time abusers or are not frequent abusers will invariably drift into that category. But some of them certainly will drift. In any case the fact remains that drug abuse is taking them off from many other constructive activities that they could have undertaken alternatively, social service not excluding. Drug pleasures (if they can be called pleasures at all) are substituting pleasures arising out of achievements in the fields of sports or academics. Passivity is getting encouraged in place of activity which has always been the hallmark of youth. How is it that a few members constituting the elite groups are able to exercise peer pressure far in excess of their numerical strength in the group ? The answer probably lies in the fact that students from relatively not so rich families consider it a privilege to be in the company of the rich specially the *nauve riche* family children. Their ways and manners are copied as they give the satisfaction of 'me too being in the elite group'. So although the rich family children are not in majority, they exercise influence far in excess of their strength in the peer group. Not everyone can afford a motor bike or a Maruti. But the one who does attracts a number of friends. Others who have lower self-esteem easily adopt such boys and girls as their role models.

While examining residential status, it was found that more hostelers were drug abusers as compared to the day scholars. It may not be possible to rule out residence in hostels but hostel life certainly needs to be made richer by way of increased facilities for co-curricular participations. The danger has to be accepted and efforts have to be made to ensure that hostels remain a drug-free zone.

Hostel wardens should be more actively involved. There is need for drug awareness campaigns along with drug scouts who should keep a watch over drugs entering the hostels. The entire organisations for prevention of drug abuse in the hostel have to be student-based rather than official-based. Students should be medically examined periodically to detect cases of drug abuse, if any, at an early stage. The war has to be fought on many fronts. The abuse of drugs is very intimately related to the availability of pocket money. The findings of high correlation between large amounts of pocket money and incidence of drug abuse are confirmed by similar studies conducted elsewhere. Khan M. Z. (1985) made congruent observations based on his study on college youth. There are proportionately more habitual users and multiple users of drug among those who are receiving large amounts of pocket money.

Family culture plays a very important role in drug abusing behaviour of college boys and girls. Drug abuse is more prevalent where parental supervision is permissive towards use of cigarettes or alcohol by their wards. The gateway drugs in course of time lead to hard drugs. Casual use is the first stage of frequent use ultimately leading to addiction if unchecked in between.

Researches confirm that lack of parental control is the most determining factor in boys and girls getting trapped into alcohol or drug abuse. (Falewicz, 1970, Wiener, 1970; Roslyn and George, 1968; Hurlock, 1974) stated that familial norms play an important role in the development of the individual.

There is some controversy about the role of low educational and occupational income level of parents *vis-a-vis* their wards getting into drug abuse. Bates *et al.* (1969) concluded that drug users belong to families having low educational and occupational levels. The findings of the study conducted by the author at Delhi University do not support these observations. Discussions with the drug abusers show that drug abuse is common both among wards coming from very deprived families as also from rich and even very rich families. It would not be safe to confine prevention or de-addiction programmes only to the economically poor sections of the society. Role imitation by young people is an accepted phenomenon. The behaviour of boys and girls included in the study was found to be significantly influenced by the attitudes of parents towards drugs. Drug abuse is a learned behaviour and where children find their parents taking drugs, they have no inhibitions in imitating their elders. Way (1970) had emphasised the influence of family members on children's drug abuse behaviour as role imitation. The findings of this study are congruent in this respect.

Uncertainty about the future was found to be an important factor operating in case of boys and girls resorting to drug abuse. As already stated, most students at universities and colleges have no specific career goals. For many of them it is just a waiting room where they have to remain till they get a job. The present lack of opportunities for employment is depressing and in many cases frustrating young boys and girls not knowing how to get over these frustrations resort to drugs. Unfortunately the colleges and universities have hardly any liaison with prospective employers. The college studies are not geared to the requirements of the prospective employers. This mismatch is one of the major frustrating causes leading to idle minds drifting into the world of drugs.

Leisure time hollowness is where possible being filled with discos. There would be nothing objectionable about young boys and girls dancing together since that is what forms part of Indian culture with its rich tradition of folk music and dances. But the discos are different. 'Dum' is an essential constituent of the disco even if it be legally not permissible.

A study by Subramanium (1980) indicated that in leisure time many college students choose to go to discos which in turn attract them towards drugs. Falewicz (1970) research suggests that lack of proper leisure time activity boosts drug-taking behaviours.

Several researches show that there is a common belief that drug-taking behaviours are related to sensuality, that certain drugs boost eroticism, induce ecstatic pleasure and can make a person have 'peak experience' which may not be common under normal circumstances (Wilson 1973). It is believed that alcohol enhances sexual enjoyment and the 'sexual powers of marijuana are unlimited' (Lewis 1973). LSD is also termed as one hallucinogen that boosts sex-sensations. The results of this study confirm the prevalence of these beliefs and attitudes among college students. In the absence of studies with a control group against whom the findings could be contrasted, it is not possible to comment upon the popularly prevailing beliefs. It would be better to stick to the medically supported belief that continued use of drugs retards sexual activity.

Moreover as Tribhuwan Kapur in his study on Indian youth (1985) writes : "...Drugs...cause complete distortion of the evaluative faculty in the mind... . In this state there is no critical faculty that could guide a person to the type of person in the opposite sex who would really be of a suitable temperament. Instead the person who is most available at the moment is taken on". The results of the study conducted by the author support the above contention as it confirms sex indulgence by drug abusers with professionals.

13

Self-esteem Structure of Drug Abusers

Self-esteem is a construct that has been formulated to summarise certain features of human behaviours. H.B. Kaplan is of the view that low self-esteem leads to decreased ability to cope with situations. It is also responsible for high anxiety, passivity, hopelessness and a deep sense of failure. Self-esteem denotes self-regarding attitudes such as self-worth, self-confidence, self-evaluation, self-love, self-acceptance etc. It is linked with the concept of personality integration relative to person's ability to react to a variety of incoming stimuli. While high self-esteem leads to effective social functioning, low self-esteem makes a person feel dependent and influenced by prevailing context. Gergen (1971) states, "The person's evaluation of esteem of himself plays a key role in determining his behaviour". The person with low self-esteem is more likely to lack self-confidence, be dependent upon others, be shy, be non-explorative and guarded to use defensive facades (Rosenberg, 1965), be unimaginative, value conformity, avoid self- analysis and use repressive defences (Linton & Graham 1959).

Keeping in view the importance of self-esteem in shaping one's personality patterns, self-esteem structure of the drug-abusers has been studied by the author. Low self-esteem leads to defensive behaviours and since the drug behaviour has been termed as defence mechanism behaviour pattern, it is important to study self-esteem patterns of drug-abusers.

Self-Perception Inventory (Adult form) developed by Soares and Soares in 1965 and revised in 1975 has been used. To measure the self-esteem only two sub-scales of the inventory *i.e.* Self-Concept Scale — how the individual sees himself as a person *i.e.* 'the real' self and Ideal Concept Scale — how individual would like to be *i.e.* 'ideal self', have been used. There are 36 items in each sub-scale composed of dichotomous traits separated by four spaces of distance in a forced choice format. The discrepancy between the two scales provides a measure of self-esteem. The higher the discrepancy, lower the self-esteem and lower the discrepancy, higher the self-esteem. High/low groups for self-esteem have been drawn by taking 30th percentile as the cut-off point. To find out the structure of self-esteem factor analysis has been done by Varimax Rotation. The following eight meaningful factors of self-esteem have emerged.

	Items	**Loadings**
Factor I	**Cheerful – Depressed**	
A.	Cheerful – Depressed	.78
B.	Even-tempered – Moody	.71
C.	Satisfied – Self-pitying	.69
D.	Optimistic – Pessimistic	.65
E.	Worthy – Unworthy	.60
Factor II	**Hopeful-Anxious**	
A.	Hopeful – Anxious	.82
B.	Contented – Worried	.79
C.	Patient – Impatient	.75
D.	Relaxed – Nervous	.71
E.	Calm – Restless	.65
F.	Deliberate – Impulsive	.55
G.	Self-controlled – Emotional	.51
H.	Tolerant – Fault-finding	.45
Factor III	**Self-confident-Insecure**	
A.	Self-confident – Insecure	.65
B.	Sociable – Shy	.62
C.	Outgoing – Withdrawn	.57
D.	Independent – Dependent	.46
Factor IV	**Accepted Rejected**	
A.	Accepted – Rejected	.75
B.	Easy going – Quick tempered	.62
C.	Enthusiastic – Indifferent	.52
D.	Considerate – Selfish	.44

Items	**Loadings**
Factor V **Self-sufficient – Easily-influenced**	
A. Self-sufficient – Easily-influenced	.69
B. Assertive – Submissive	.63
C. Alert – Absent-minded	.53
D. Well-adjusted – Poorly-adjusted	.42
Factor VI **Mature – Immature**	
A. Mature – Immature	.83
B. Good-natured – Critical	.68
C. Tough – Sensitive	.54
Factor VII **Trusting – Suspicious**	
A. Trusting – Suspicious	.73
B. Adaptable – Rigid	.66
C. Cooperative – Anti-social	.59
Factor VIII **Masculine – Feminine**	
A. Masculine – Feminine	.77
B. Poised – Ashamed	.73
C. Creative – Conforming	.61
D. Responsible – Frivolous	.51
E. Persevering – Quitting	.46

The above factors have been named as per their highest loadings on the scale. Their loadings were lower on other scales.

Results of the study show that drug abusers, in general, were found to have low self-esteem. (Mean 3.91 and SD 1.12)

↑ 3.91

0 1 2 3 4 5 6

High self-esteem Low self-esteem

Table 13.1
Percentage Distribution of Drug Abusers with High-Low Self-esteem

HSE	LSE	Total
31%	69%	100

The table shows that 69 per cent drug abusers had low self-esteem. It shows that there is a wide gap in these drug-abusers, 'real' and 'ideal self'. Only 31 per cent felt congruency in their real and ideal self *i.e.* have high self-esteem. The results confirm the earlier researches which postulate that there is a direct relationship between low self-esteem and drug abuse (Blum and Richards 1979; Jessor, 1975, Wechsler, 1976).

Factors of Self-esteem and Percentage Distribution of Drug Abusers with High-Low Self-esteem.

Table 13.2

Factor I	**Cheerful** –	**Depressed**
	HSE	LSE
	43	57

On the factor of cheerful-depressed, only 43 per cent students reflected having high self-esteem and 57 per cent had low self-esteem. This shows that drug abusers have incongruency in their real and ideal self on this factor. The scores of real self show that high self-esteem group perceives himself as cheerful while low self-esteem group as being depressed. The findings show that drug abusers with low self-esteem on this component of self-esteem are not happy-go-lucky type. These findings are in support of previous researches that depression is both the cause and the effect of drug abuse. Rado (1933) stated that drug addicts by and large suffer from 'ego-frustration' which is a cause for acute depression. Yost (1954) findings show that drug-taking behaviour is correlated with frustrations, indecisiveness and unhappiness.

Table 13.3

Factor II	**Hopeful** –	**Anxious**
	HSE	LSE
	23%	77%

Self-esteem measured on the dimension of Hopeful-Anxious shows that seventy-seven per cent drug abusers had low self-esteem on this dimension while 23 per cent had high self-esteem. Scores on real self on this component of self-esteem show that low self-esteem group is anxiety-prone as compared to the group with high self-esteem that may be a cause of their drug taking behaviour. Mc Dill (1965) stated that in every addicted personality there is excessive anxiety and a lack of psychic tolerance for anxiety. Other researches also indicate that psychic conditions of anxiety are related to drug use. (Blumenfield and Glickman, 1967; Lewis and Albert, 1969).

Table 13.4

Factor III	**Self-Confident**	–	**Insecure**
	HSE		LSE
	63%		37%

The table shows that drug abusers have high self-esteem as measured on the component of self-confident — insecure. Sixty three per cent of drug abusers had high self-esteem on this dimension while 37 per cent had low self-esteem. This reflects that the high self-esteem group on this component had less discrepancy in his perception of 'real self' and 'ideal self' as compared to the group with low self-esteem. The scores of real-self on this dimension reflect that high self-esteem group felt self-confident. These results do not support the previous findings that show that addicts are less confident and insecure (Gilbert and Lombardi, 1967) but confirm the findings of Khan M. Z. (1985) that it is not the feeling of insecurity but that of security which increases the likelihood of drug use. The occurrence of self-confidence in the student population of drug abusers may be due to the reason that they show self-confidence as a 'self-defence mechanism'. Some projective techniques to measure the personality may be used in future researches to get a clear picture.

Table 13.5

Factor IV	**Accepted**	–	**Rejected**
	HSE		LSE
	81%		19%

Self-esteem measured on this component shows that 81 per cent drug abusers had high self-esteem on this dimension of self-esteem and 19 per cent had low self-esteem. 'Real self' of high self-esteem drug abusers show that they felt themselves accepted.

The results in the previous chapter show that the most important factor that leads to students taking drugs is the peer-group pressure. The result of the component of 'accepted-rejected' may be seen in the light of this phenomenon. The drug-abusers had high self-esteem on this dimension, maybe because they felt accepted in their own 'peer-group'.

Table 13.6

Factor V	**Self-Sufficient**	–	**Easily Influenced**
	HSE		LSE
	39%		61%

Thirty-nine per cent drug abusers had high self-esteem measured on self-sufficient-easily influenced component and 61 per cent had low self-esteem on this dimension. Scores of 'real-self' show that high self-esteem group perceived itself as being self-sufficient while low-esteem group felt itself as being easily influenced. The persons with the personality who find it difficult to say 'no', submit easily to pressures. Being easily influenced by others is one of the important causes which drives people into the drug net.

Table 13.7

Factor VI	**Mature**	–	**Immature**
	HSE		LSE
	26%		74%

The table shows that 26 per cent drug abusers showed congruency in their 'real' and 'ideal' self on this dimension and 74 per cent perceived a vast gap between their 'real' and 'ideal' self. In order to play adult matured roles, the gap between 'real' and 'ideal' widens and drugs might be used as 'cowardice' to cover up this gap.

Table 13.8

Factor VII	**Trusting**	–	**Suspicious**
	HSE		LSE
	39%		61%

Thirty-nine per cent drug abusers had high self-esteem as measured on 'Trusting-Suspicious' component and 61 per cent had low self-esteem. The scores of real self show that low self-esteem group is suspicious in nature. This may be one of the reasons for students being in the drug net. Suspicion of being neglected in the group could compel students to take to drugs.

Table 13.9

Factor VIII	**Masculine**	–	**Feminine**
	HSE		LSE
	64%		36%

Self-esteem measured on 'masculine-feminine' component show that 64 per cent drug abusers had high self-esteem on this dimension and 36 per cent had low self-esteem. Real-self scores show that persons with high self-esteem felt themselves as being 'masculine'. This again calls for the Self-defence Mechanism theory. Though the data has not been analysed for males and females separately but on this dimension the reactions of female have been observed. The female population of drug abusers feel themselves as being 'masculine'. It may be a denial of the prevailing sex-role stereotypes. Masculinity is positively valued in the society as compared to 'femininity'. In order to prove their worth females perceive themselves as having 'masculine' characteristics. This is also one of the reasons that prompts women to take drugs just as their male counterparts do.

Findings of the study show that in general drug-abusers suffer from lower levels of self-esteem. Self-esteem measured on factors shows that on some factors such as on the components of self-confident insecure, accepted, rejected and masculine-faminine, drug-abusers show high self-esteem which may be a pseudo-esteem or a defensive behaviour. A more indepth study is needed to explore the personality characteristics that are directly related to use of drugs among college students taking into consideration samples of drug-abusers as well as non-users.

14

Emerging Vulnerable Groups

The war between traffickers and pushers and the enforcement agencies goes on unabated. As the enforcement agencies tighten their control mechanisms leading to large-scale seizures and arrests, the drug lords also keep on modifying their operational strategies. They have now started looking for pushers among groups that would be least suspected. Women and children are now the soft targets.

Women and Drugs

Drug abuse among women has registered alarming increase over the past few decades. A survey conducted by the National Institute of Mental Health (USA) revealed that drug abuse was the second most common psychiatric disorder among women aged 18 to 24 (Robins *et al* 1984). The drug-taking behaviour of females in India shows that use of nicotine in the form of chewing tobacco (often taken along with traditional 'pan') and smoking beedis/cigarettes are very common. Women belonging to economically weaker sections of the society mostly smoke beedis. Middle class women in many regions of the country are strongly addicted to chewing tobacco. Cigarettes are becoming increasingly popular among the elite classes. It is no longer uncommon to see elite women smoking cigarettes.

A study conducted in Calcutta by Mr. J. N. Mondal of Calcutta University revealed that out of total addict population of Calcutta, 4 per cent were women hailing from upper middle class families. 'Modernity' seems to be the driving force in their cases. The study revealed that average age of women heroin addicts was 27 years and in case of alcoholics, it was 35 years. Sixty per cent of women heroin addicts were married. The report states that "confinement at home and inability to receive any kind of change for the better are liable to make women apathetic and schizoid. The present trend of consumerism, the dowry system and its consequent repercussions, separation and divorce may lead to increasing rate of drug addiction among women."

Interviews with college girls in Delhi, who either smoke or take alcohol, show that these practices have got associated with 'liberation'. Advertisement of cigarettes such as 'Cigarettes specially for women (slim line) or Gin as 'Lady's drink' often tempt girls to these products. These advertisements sell a high life-style and the girls fall for it.

Girls also go in for drugs or alcohol as an expression of hidden anger towards authority to which they have been traditionally subjected. They also have a feeling that refusal to take drinks or alcohol is going to get them branded as old fashioned. One girl confided that she didn't approve of drinking alcohol in the first instance. However, she was in a group party where everybody had a round. She was offered one, while her friends persuaded her to accept it or else the host would mind it. She yielded to the pressure and now she has no inhibitions left.

The use of drugs and disco culture seems to bear strong correlation. Everyday more and more girls are getting tempted to explore the euphoric heights promised by use of drugs.

It has also been found in the sample study that girls from business families are becoming more prone to drug temptations. They have more pocket money at their disposal and their families are less restrictive. Both factors contribute to their being greater prone to drug abuse.

Girls from families of defence services officers also have little or no inhibitions about smoking or drinking alcohol. They see it being used at home as a part of socialising with no stigma attached to their use.

A recent phenomenon observed during the study was that girls as well as boys from families of politicians were getting into the net in increasing numbers. The father, at least in their case, had no time for family communications and money was relatively easy on hand.

Drug pushers see women as their prospective customers. Doctors and social workers, on the other hand, are worried about the consequences of drug abuse among women in more than one dimension. Women, by virtue of their characteristic physiological conditions, are more prone to damage by use of drugs. Apart from the individual, drugs affect the children borne by them.

Female alcoholics have been found to be suffering from menstural abnormalities, decreased sexual characteristics and sterility. Women smokers give birth to children who are underweight and who may develop heart and lung diseases.

Use of alcohol and other drugs hinders development of normal intellect among children. Tobacco use, during pregnancy, is reported to induce abortions in increasing numbers.

A Women Drug Research Project (USA) found that the female addict, when compared with non-addict counterpart, appeared lower in self-esteem, higher in reported symptoms of depression, and anxiety, more open to development of relationship, lower in masculinity and higher in assertiveness.

Getting into addiction of drugs is a very perverse way for establishing equality or liberation. Even ordinary women can establish their identity if they take up problems of illicit or otherwise sale of liquor as in the case of women in village Nahri (Sonepat-Haryana). They succeeded in forcing the closure of a liquor vend near their village much to the happiness of their families. Similar efforts have been made in Kohima by Naga Mothers' Association. Manipur Women are also up in arms against peddlers and addicts.

These isolated efforts need to be co-ordinated through a national organisation with effective leadership with its branches spread into every village or locality. These will go a long way in giving average women a chance to establish themselves and also supplement the efforts being made by other officials and non-government organisations to combat the drug menace.

For the elite women, it would suffice to say that a woman as Prime Minister of a country, a judge of the Supreme Court, an Everest conqueror, a channel swimmer or an Inspector-General of Prisons reacting with and reforming a thousand hardened criminals is much more liberated than the socialite puffing cigarettes or taking alcohol in a club or its psuedo-imitation.

Drug Abuse among Street Children

Large-scale industrialisation has led to uncontrolled migration of rural children to urban centres where notwithstanding extreme exploitation, job opportunities do exist for them. These children have no homes to fall back upon and invariably live on the streets. According to a WHO study, almost 100 per cent of these street children living in the cities of Montreal and Toronto were found to be regularly using alcohol and other drugs. A very significant proportion of street children in the metropolitan cities like Bombay were also found to be using alcohol and drugs.

The WHO study was conducted on substance abuse in ten cities around the world. It was found that the substances commonly used by street children were those that were cheap and easily available. These included tobacco, alcohol, cannabis (ganja), solvents and pharmaceuticals. The study covered 550 children in the cities of Alexandria, Cairo, Lusaka, Manila, Mexico City, Rio de Janeiro, Tegucigalpa, Bombay, Montreal and Toronto.

The street children were found to be actively associated with illicit manufacture and trafficking of drugs. They were found involved in the production of cocaine and trafficking of cannabis and heroin. Many of these children were sexually exploited at a very young age. Instances also came to light where the street children, besides being used for drug trafficking, were being used to carry out subversive activities by terrorist groups.

The exodus from villages to cities is not a recent phenomenon. However, adverse economic situation in the rural areas, political upheavals and social unrest in some societies, increasing family disintegration and in some cases natural disasters have boosted the exodus of children from rural homes to urban streets. In some cases it was found that the children were born on the streets while most others came from poverty-stricken families in the backward villages. There were orphans too among the population studied by the WHO.

The reasons why children came to streets were not always economic. In a number of cases they came to the city streets having fled away from their homes where they were being physically and even sexually abused. The girls among them had to face worst exploitation.

The Director of the WHO programme on substance abuse Mr. Hans Emblad felt that "this was a global problem and had to be addressed globally". He had apprehensions that the problem would take even tragic turns damaging more and more young lives unless a strong network of influential individuals and agencies was formulated in place to work with street children.

The incidence of AIDS is further compounding the problem. It has been estimated that by early 2000 A.D., in USA alone there would be 16 million orphaned by the deadly disease. The Street Kids International and other UN agencies are proposed to be involved in rehabilitation projects besides a number of government and voluntary agencies.

In India one comes across children working under the most inhuman and unhygienic conditions in city 'dhabas', on the pavements as shoe-shine boys and beggars at red light crossings. They do odd jobs during the day and spend the night on the pavements or in slums often under the shelter of the people for whom they work during the day. The employers keep an eye on their movements lest they escape from their clutches.

Interviews with a number of street children by the author in the city of Delhi have revealed that drug trafficking is a very common occupation among them. Many of these children join their parents in the illicit trade. Since their parents are also involved, they have no prick of conscience or feeling of guilt. They have no contrastive models of good conduct before them. In a way, they feel they are being helpful to their parents. These children were found to be familiar with the use of drugs like heroin and smack, their parents being regular users. Drug trafficking is the normal business of the families.

The children are used partly because they are less likely to be suspected in trafficking and mostly because there is no other option before the parents or the children.

Raju (not the real name) aged 12 revealed the following during the course of the interview · "We are three families coming from Bihar. We were landless labourers but now there is no work in the fields there. Even when my parents worked on the farms, there was never enough for us to eat. So we took the train to Delhi. There are many people from our side. After sometime we were able to find a place on the pavement. By way of occupation we beg in the fashionable shopping centres. Sometimes some of us sell fruits. But there is not enough money in that business. We find it much better to sell smack. The foreigner sahib gives us good money. My father and mother both take smack. I too take it to feel big. My parents do not mind it. Where is the time?"

The sale and purchase of drugs are common at the pan shops and the dhabas, the children being used as carriers.

Yet another boy had the following story to tell.

"I used to work at a tea shop. I had to work till late in the night. Later I used to sleep outside the shop. But I knew many a truck drivers stopped there and got packets from my employer at night. First, I did not know what these packets contained. One day my employer gave me a packet to be delivered to a truck driver. I was apprehended by a policeman while carrying that packet. My employer disowned me, saying, 'I don't know anything about this boy. The truck driver accused me of selling the packet. I was taken to the police station and given a severe thrashing. I remained in lock-up for two days and then I was let off. My employer was nowhere when I was in trouble. But now he forced me to work again or else he threatened me to hand over to the police once again. The police did nothing to my employer or the truckwallah. The business goes on as usual. I am very terrified but have nowhere to go."

It has come to light that street children are exposed to a very unusual risk apart from being used as drug traffickers. *The Times of India* (March 14, 1994) reported that the eunuch gangs in Delhi (there are about 12,000 to 15,000 of them) would drug street children and castrate them to join their ranks. The children castrated were used for male prostitution. The fact came to light when 30 such children escaped from the highly organised gang. The eunuchs in the city are not cases of a natural genetic flukee as one would normally imagine. It is estimated that 95 per cent of them are castrated boys befriended by eunuchs and lured into the world of drugs from where they are forced into a much more vicious life.

The WHO study identified strategies that could be effectively utilised for combating the menace of street children being used in drug trafficking and in course being turned to drugs. Drop-in centres have been planned for the street children in Bombay. Other strategies include involving the children in constructive enterprises like brick making (in Lusaka) and carpentry (in Tegucigalpa). Voluntary organisations that work with street children are to be strengthened as a part of the strategy to keep the street children off the drug racketeers.

Tegucigalpa has evolved a comprehensive package to tackle the problem. Health and welfare agencies tie up with the community and plan jointly for the street children. Others involved in the programme include peers and volunteers, professionals and street educators.

Both women and street children are soft targets. They are being lured into the world of drugs both as abusers and pushers. The situation is becoming serious and alarming day by day.

It is not enough that the governments legislate or international forums draw up elaborate plans for drug prevention and control. Individual societies have to create contrastive models by setting up and encouraging institutions where women and children already in the drug net or those most prone to getting trapped can look forward to constructive opportunities for a fuller and healthy life. Any society that wakes up only after the damage has been done would be paying a heavy price for its indifference. Many a cancer can be treated if detected and treated early. Drugs are no less dangerous but equally receptive to early treatment.

15

Myths and False Beliefs

Myths abound about the wonders that drugs can create in human lives. There may be no scientific basis for the presumptions nor any established precedents about drugs having produced wonders but that hardly matters to the drug abuser who is out to rationalise his conduct. These prevalent myths and false beliefs adversely hinder the success of prevention programmes.

During counselling sessions, the author came across a wide variety of such myths prevalent among young men and women, specially the college-going population. Some of the commonly used cliches are being reproduced below along with the answers given by the author during counselling sessions. Some of the answers brought forth positive responses and made the students introspect. The following format would be specially useful to the readers who may nurse any such myth about drug abuse.

"*I am very strong. I can get out of it any time I want to ?*"

Fact : The fact that one has been tempted to take it once is proof enough that he is not so strong as claimed. Drugs destroy inner strength. Once under the influence of drugs, one is not the same person who boasted about his inner strength. It is like getting into a mouse trap, very easy to get in – very hard to get out.

How does one socialise without drinks ? It is so common specially in business deals :

Fact : Socialising doesn't have much to do with drinks. A number of very senior army officers do not take alcohol and this never comes in their way of socialising with the highest dignitaries. As a matter of fact, high dignitaries always show respect to those who do not take drinks. It is only if one is half willing that social pressure works. The same is true about business situations. The success or otherwise of a business deal is determined by its perceived profitability. No amount of drinks can persuade a shrewd businessman to clinch a deal unless he is satisfied that it would be financially profitable. In all high-level parties, there is provision for those who do not take alcohol.

It's part of the community rituals :

Fact : Some tribal societies do celebrate with alcohol. Gradually, as they are getting into the mainstream of education, their social customs are changing. The community elders may be addicts. But they would take pride in the fact that their next generation is keeping out of drugs. The pressure is not from the community seniors specially if one is educated. It is one's own choice for getting into the temptation.

Alcohol is not a drug. A round of beer or wine is hardly going to make one an addict :

Fact : The difficulty is that once one initiates himself into the world of drugs or alcohol, one step leads to another. Beer leads to whisky and whisky to yet more harder drinks. All addicts started with the conviction that they would not get trapped. In fact alcohol is a drug that interferes with the body and brain functions.

Drugs and alcoholic drinks have been part of human society since ancient times :

Fact : There have been perverts in the past as they are in the present. However, they cannot be models to emulate. At no time have any worthwhile contributions to social progress come from addicts. Best achievements have always come from people who had single-minded devotion to their work and did not get digressed by use of drugs or alcohol.

Some poets and musicians are known for their addiction and also their contributions. They all died young. There are many more superior to them who have lived longer to make much bigger and lasting contributions.

It puts you at par with other elite sections of the society :

Fact : No one distinctly superior in status, professional or monetary, would be willing to clink glasses except with people of equal social status. Everyone likes to socialise in his own group. What one gets by way of status after being 'high' is just self-deception.

It makes sex more enjoyable :

Fact : Drugs make one feel uninhibited. However, they have very adverse physical reactions. They decrease the sex urge in the long run and retard what is normally regarded as manliness. Sex is best enjoyed by couples in perfect health. Alcohol and drugs are the very antithesis of good health. Wilson (1973) found that alcohol addiction is one of the primary causes of 'secondary impotence'.

A little amount of alcohol helps in digestion :

Fact : Human body has its own stimulants where needed or necessary. The digestive system produces its own juices and secretions needed for effective digestion of food. Alcohol only disturbs the normal functioning. If a person has digestive problems, the solution lies in checking out on his menu and lifestyle.

It helps concentration :

Fact : Alcohol and drugs retard manipulative sensibilities. As soon as the percentage of alcohol in the blood crosses the safe limit, a ringing feeling sets in, which hinders concentration. Once a person is high, he loses control over his mental faculties. Thus, the time available for serious work is severely reduced. Hangover follows and during that time too no worthwhile work is possible.

I can drown my sorrows and frustration in drinks :

Fact : This is like the legendary ostrich burying its head in the sand when a storm is approaching. No one is free from failures. Frustrations and grief are essential parts of human existence. Drugs do not change anything. One's own efforts can. Drugs do not ease stress. They create many more problems that ultimately add to the distress. There is the perpetual feeling of guilt that dampens the self-confidence to fight against adverse conditions.

Drugs sometimes act by disconnecting the brain from the part of the body causing 'pain'. That is like the fire station phone being disconnected from the site of fire. The right thing would be that factors causing pain are remedied. Drugs, in the long run, make the cognitive faculties handicapped. They are incapable of 'relieving pain' or 'eliminating' distress.

I can compete better with a little pep :

Fact : Many a career of world famous sportsmen has been ruined by drugs. There are very strict rules about debarring players from competitive sports if the slightest amount of drug is detected. Simple drugs like ephedrine can be detected months after the player has stopped taking them.

The world's best players and sportsmen and women insist on a very controlled life totally free from use of drugs or peps of any kind.

It puts me on the top of the world at least for some time : In any case I know I would never reach the top :

Fact : One can never be sure about not reaching the top. It is just a matter of a right break which in all cases comes once a person has acquired perfection in his job or trade. The position one acquires in his own trade through achievement of perfection is permanent. Drug addiction on the other hand destroys every possible chance of ever reaching the top.

How else does one celebrate ?

Fact : Champagne is only one way to celebrate. Moreover, celebration does not mean getting out of senses. Indian societies, even primitive and tribal, have many ways of celebration — through group singing and dancing even without the use of alcohol. A large number of celebrations are in fact associated with religious rituals and preceded by very austere meals — devoid of even meat.

If future is so uncertain why bother about it. Have a nice time.

Fact : Future is only an extension of present. If one chooses to be wreckless today, disaster is certain in future. Anyone careful and prudent today can look forward to a future with hope.

"The capacity of drugs to overtake ordinary persons is much higher than that of the addicts to overcome them. The only way to defeat them is to keep them very far from the life's routine."

16

Towards a Drug-free India

As one views the drug scene all around, it is a vast stretch of darkness. Are drugs going to wipe off all that human efforts and ingenuity have created over the centuries ? Will they prove to be humanity's curse like plague or small pox ? The answer lies in the query itself.

The war against drugs has to be fought to win. The Chinese got over the national curse of opium addiction through sustained efforts. Gujarat in India can do without excise revenues earned through sale of liquor. It is not the most backward state either. These examples confirm that where people want to do things they certainly can. Where does one start ? Efforts by the mightiest powers like America seem to fail. Does a country like India has any chance of succeeding ? As to the first question the answer is "the individual ? And if success is achieved at that level, the answer to the second question cannot be anything other than YES."

It has been established that the most important preventive step against getting into the temptation of drugs is the individual's personality. Nothing can trap an individual who is confident about his worth and has before him a goal to be achieved. For the one fired with ambition and zeal there is no idleness and no surplus energy to waste out in drugs. It is not easy to create a social order in which each individual is fired with zeal for a cause. It is not impossible either. Where societies have before them larger issues to tackle that encompasses the entire groups, people feel involved. They can take delight in social achievements even when their personal achievements may be frustrating.

In India, the commonly used gateway drugs were beedis, cigarettes and chewing tobacco. Other drugs included alcoholic drinks, bhang, charas and opium. Many more drugs have now emerged on the scene. Their sale is more through illegal channels than through legalised vends. Under these circumstances, the preventive authorities have to be well familiar with the various drugs and derivatives, their slang names and sources of supply. The illicit drugs distribution network is spread over global frontiers There is the Golden Triangle in the East and the Golden Crescent in the North-West. These two are also the areas with maximum threats of insurgency and terrorism. Political solutions to problems such as Naga insurgency or Kashmir militancy can no longer be divorced from drug smuggling which is the source of armaments availability to the insurgents groups.

It is no linger enough that the preventive and enforcement officials know about the drugs and the symptoms of drug abusers. This man-made curse which threatens to disfigure the beautiful world created by God is gradually sneaking into our homes. As parents, we should be able to note behavioural changes in our wards and make sure that they are not because of his or her having got trapped in the drug net.

A number of socio-economic factors influence drug abuse in the society. It is not possible to identify any single factor since they act in combination often one influencing the other. In developing societies drugs are being regarded as a symbol of modernity. The developed societies are getting trapped as their youth achieve most pleasures of life at a very early age. Permissiveness and frustration of achievement act together in their case driving them to the world of drugs that pretends to take them into unseen realms of life.

One factor that seems most effective against drug abuse is the 'integrated family'. India is fortunate in this respect. It is very important that this asset is not allowed to be frittered away in the race for modernisation (read Westernisation). It can exercise the most dominating influence in preventing children from drifting into drug abuse.

Where families have opportunities for activities like 'play together' or 'pray together', the child grows up with a feeling of being wanted. The achievement may be modest, yet if it is taken note of by the parents, the child grows into a confident personality. He or she doesn't feel isolated or lonely.

A very heavy responsibility rests on the parents. They are the role models for the youngsters. If they want their children to keep away from drugs, they themselves will have to be away from them. The type of entertainments to which the children are exposed have to be carefully determined by the parents in the initial stages. Boys and girls who develop healthy hobbies and leisure time activities are least prone to getting into the drug net.

The West is learning at great cost that nothing can substitute the role of family so far as shaping attitudes among boys and girls is concerned. In India we have to balance modernisation with our cultural heritages. The individual who is wanting in self-confidence is easily suggestible. If he gets into a group where drugs are the in-thing, the chances are that he will get into the drug net like the rest of his peers.

The role of family and peer pressure have been highly stressed by a number of studies including the one by this author. The former can act as the best armour. The latter acts as the greatest promoter of drug culture.

The prevalent myths about what drugs can do need to be shattered. Drugs cannot establish an individual's identity. At best they can retard whatever growth might be taking place in an expression of individual's creativity.

If that be so, drug prevention to be effective needs to be organised at various levels. While the family keeps a tab over the individual member getting trapped, the society has to raise a number of institutions that would supplement family efforts and also help those who inspite of the family check get into drug abuse. Community based campaigns need to be coordinated with similar efforts at work places, schools and colleges. Both the government and non-government organisations need to work in close collaboration. Where such collaboration exists, the results have been remarkable.

Drug addiction treatment is as much a part of society as treatment for epidemics, contagious diseases or other illnesses. There is illness even in the most hygienic societies. Similarly there would be addicts in the most regulated societies. A number of therapies are since available for treatment of drug addicts. The doctor and the psychologist working together can achieve results which have to be followed up by social workers and family members for total rehabilitation. The de-addicted individual need not be shunned or ostracised. He needs special care and attention like the convalescing patient. Relapse has to be prevented or else all efforts at de-addiction come to naught.

There are a number of self-help techniques that can help the addicts in getting over their cravings and help in de-addiction efforts. These techniques need to be publicised and disseminated through various media. The individual must learn how to cope with failures in real life. He should be able to say 'NO' when he feels so and not be overtaken by what others will think. Such attitudes cannot be developed overnight. The family, the school and the community have to act together.

The family should help the individuals in setting life goals. The schools would provide facilities for games. It is on the playfield that one learns the most important lesson that one cannot always win. Also that even if one lost a match, the game has to be played again the next day. The community can provide a forum for expression of creative talent. Community centres can also act as physical fitness centres.

There are difficulties both at the national and international levels so far as drug prevention is concerned. The international agencies are already involved. What is needed is support from individual societies. International agencies do not have the teeth to fight the highly organised mafias. That effort has to come from individual nations. They have to stand up to pressures from their own armament manufacturer lobbies who trade with the smugglers across international borders. Drug abuse among the college-going population is becoming an increasing menace. Established value systems are getting eroded. There is need for major restructuring of school and college environments. The idleness component has to be specially taken care of.

Some social discipline will have to be enforced if colleges have to be temples of learning rather than drug joints with occasional classes not necessarily compulsory. Colleges have to be institutions where opportunities exist for developing high self-esteem. It is not simple but no other social institution is more capable for performing that essential social function.

Women and street children are some of the more vulnerable groups. They are being dragged into the drug net both as prospective customers and as traffickers and peddlers. Special efforts have to be made since drug abuse among women has very far-reaching adverse effects on the generation yet to be born.

In India, the problem of drug abuse is still within manageable limits. There is the added advantage of strong family ties. Most Indian societies are still adverse to drugs hard or soft. These advantages should not be allowed to be frittered away. There are examples from developed societies. They allowed the institution of family to become ineffective. The results are there for everyone to see. India must not lose its uniqueness in its quest for economic prosperity.

Annexure A

NIDA Prevention Programme at Workplace

NIDA operates a toll-free Drug Abuse Information and Treatment Referral Hotline to provide drug-related information to the general public, facilitate the placement of drug abusers in treatment programmes and to acquaint those affected by the drug use of a friend or family member (*i.e.*, significant other) with much-needed support groups and/or services in their area.

The National Clearinghouse for Alcohol and Drug Information (NCADI)

Box 2345, Rockville MD 20852,
1-800-729-6686 or
(301) 468-2600

NCADI is a national drug and alcohol information resource that distributes the latest research results, popular press and scholarly journal articles, videos, prevention curricula, and programme descriptions. Information specific to workplace drug abuse issues is included.

Videotape Series

NIDA has developed a four-part videotape series suitable for supervisor and employee education. The first tape, 'Drugs at Work' describes the costs of drug use in the workplace and provides information for developing effective drug-free work place programmes. The second tape, 'Getting Help' describes the value of an EAP to the comprehensive drug-free workplace programme. 'Drug Testing : Handle with Care,' the third tape, describes the options available in designing the drug testing component of a comprehensive workplace drug abuse programme. The fourth tape, 'Finding Solutions', offers education and prevention strategies for responding to drug abuse in the workplace, emphasising personal, workplace and community responsibilities. The videotape series is available from the National Clearinghouse for Alcohol and Drug Information (NCADI).

NIDA PUBLICATIONS

While supplies last, the following publications are available at no cost from NCADI.

Strategic Planning for Workplace Drug Abuse Programmmes (1987).

A guide to help employers through the process of planning and organising workplace drug abuse programmes. The guide addresses the responsibilities, needs and rights of both employees and companies in responding to drug abuse, and contains sample programmes. (62 pp.)

Model Plan for a Comprehensive Drug-free Workplace Programme (1989).

Originally developed to serve as the guide to Federal agencies in their development of drug-free workplace programmes, it has been published as a useful model for the private sector. It includes all components needed for an effective comprehensive programme : a clearly articulated written policy; supervisor training; employee education; an EAP; and provisions for identification of illegal drug abusers, including drug testing on a controlled and carefully monitored basis. (62 pp.)

Guidelines for the Development and Assessment of a Comprehensive Federal Employee Assistance Programme (1988).

Presents the essential core components of a comprehensive Federal EAP; it is also recommended for use in the private sector. The guidelines provide a framework from which to design, implement, operate, and evaluate a comprehensive EAP. The guidelines include a monitoring tool which can aid in assessing the EAP's capacity for and availability of relevant services. (33 pp.)

Drug Abuse Curriculum for Employee Assistance Programme Professionals (1989).

Designed as a training programme for EAP professionals to upgrade their knowledge and skills in responding to employees with drug abuse problems. The curriculum covers the topics of pharmacology; the physical, psychological, and behavioural effects of drugs; client assessment; case management; supervisor training; and organisational interventions and assessment procedures for drug abuse programming. (531 pp.)

To obtain copies of these and other publications, contact The National Clearing House for Alcohol and Drug Information (NCADI) P.O. Box 2345, Rockville MD 20852, 1-800-729-6686 or (301) 468-2600.

Annexure B

VOLUNTARY ORGANISATIONS, DE-ADDICTION CENTRES AND AFTER CARE CENTRES

(Funded by Ministry of Welfare — Govt. of India.)

Name and Address of the Voluntary Organisation	Name & Address of the Centre	
	Counselling	**De-addiction**
ANDHRA PRADESH		
Association for Social Health in India, State Branch, Hyderabad.	ASHI, Jagriti 10-4-5/9/2, 2nd Floor, Humayun Nagar, Hyderabad.	
ASSAM		
Association for Social Health in India, Assam State Branch, Guwahati.	Aswash, near Assam Tribune Press, Silpukhuri, Guwahati.	
BIHAR		
Association for Social Health in India, Bihar Branch, Chandra Nilayam Building, R.K. Avenue, Patna.	Kayakalap, Sachivalaya Colony, Kankar Bagh, Patna.	
Bihar Rehabilitation and Welfare Institute, Jagadamba Bhavan, G-4, People's Co-operative Colony, Kankar Bagh, Patna.		Health Restoration Services, P.O. Garh Nokhar Rohtas.
Home for Mentally Retarded and Psychological Sufferers, K-118, Hanuman Nagar, Kankar Bagh, Patna.	Nishedhalaya, Keora Purba Buxar.	Nishedhhalaya De-addiction and De-toxitication Centre, Opp. K-116, Hanuman Nagar, Kankar Bagh, Patna.

Pandit Bachan Pandey,
Mahila Vikas Sansthan,
Bankata, P.O.- Debhwa,
Distt. Gopalganj.

Aushadhi Durupyoga
Roktham Paramarsh
Sah-Upchar Kendra,
Thakur Mansion
Bhavan,
Shayam Chitramandir,
Cinema Road,
Gopal Ganj.

Youth Mobilisation for
National Advancement,
Prabhayan, Budha Colony,
Patna.

Disha, Pratibhalok,
Behind Himgiri
Bhawan, Anandpuri,
Patna.

GOA

Andre Faria Memorial Forum,
Pooja Mahal, First Floor,
Ward No. 10, Khorlim,
Mapusa, Goa.

Association for Social Health
in India,
Goa State Branch,
Asha Mahal,
Goa.

i) Community-
Counselling
Centre, near St.
Michael Church,
Anjuna Bardez,
North Goa.
ii) Community
Counselling
Centre (South Goa),
Almira Apartments,
1st Floor,
Erasmo Carvalho Street,
Margao Salcette,
South Goa.

Asha Bhawan, 33, Damodem,
Tivim,
P.O. Bardez, Goa.

Dilkhush Building,
2nd Floor, near
Municipal Corporation,
Mapusa, Goa.

GUJARAT

Gujarat Kelvani Trust, S.V.
College Compound, Reflief
Road,
Ahmedabad.

Naya Rasta, Prerna
Mangal
Prabhat Trust, Opp. St.
Xavier High School,
Ahmedabad.

De-addiction-
cum-Rehabili-
tation centre ,
Naya Jeevan
Mangal Prabhat
Trust Bldg.
Mirzapur,
Ahmedabad.

Indian Council of Social Welfare, Gujarat State Branch, Municipal Bal Bhavan, Paldi, Ahmedabad.	Naya Jeevan Municipal Bal Bhavan, Behind Paldi Bus Stand, Paldi, Ahmedabad.	
Nashabandhi Mandal, Gujarat, Opp. Multi Storey Bldg., Bhadra, Ahmedabad.	i) Nashabandhi Mandal, Bechadrdas Hospital, Jordan Road, Chakla, Ahmedabad.	i) De-Addiction-cum - Rehabilitation Centre, Shiva Nand Mission Compound Veer Nagar, Rajkot.
	ii) Navprabhat Vyasan Muktikendra, Civil Hospital Campus, Petlad Road, Nadiad.	Parivartan Vyasan Mukti Kendra, Old Civil Hospital Compound, Chowk Bazar, Surat.
Rachnatmak Ahbigam Trust, 'Hardik' Prerana, Park Society, Opp. L.G. Hospital, Maninayar, Ahmedabad.	Nai Roshani Counselling Centre for Drug Addicts, Pratap Kunj, Behind Jain Dera Sar, Kareli Bag, Baroda.	
S.C. Patel Trust Cancer Research Institute & De-addiction Centre, A/1, Mudra Complex, Ellore Park, Baroda.		S.C. Patel De-addiction Centre, Mudra Complex, Ellora Park, Baroda.

HARYANA

Association for Social Health in India, Chandigarh Branch, Chandigarh.	Haryana Jagriti Kendra Drug Counselling Centre, 597/22 Jhang Colony, Vijay Park, Rohtak.	

Haryana State Council For Child Welfare, Bal Vikas Bhavan, 650, Sector 16-D, Chandigarh.	i) Counselling Centre for Drug Addicts, Bal Bhavan, Near Bus Stand, Ambala. ii) Counselling Centre for Drug Addicts, Kothi-21-A, Faridabad. iii) Counselling Centre for Drug Addicts, Youth Hostel, G.T. Road, Pipli, Kurukshetra. iv) Counselling Centre for Drug Addicts Sector-9-173, Panchkula. v) Counselling Centre for Drug Addicts, Bal Bhavan, Barnala Road, Sirsa.	i) De-addiction Centre, Kothi No. 1106, Sector IV, Gurgaon. ii) De-addiction-cum- Rehabilitation Centre, Kothi, No. 86, Sector-17, Panchkula.
Indian Red Cross Society Distt. Branch, Red Cross Bhavan, Sector - 14, Faridabad.		
Indian Red Cross Society Distt. Branch, Hissar.	Red Cross Counselling Centre for Drug Addicts, Railway Road, Hissar.	Drug De-addiction Centre, Red Cross Bhavan, Sector-14, Faridabad.
Indian Red Cross Society Distt. Branch, Karnal.	Counselling Centre for Drug Addicts, Red Cross Road, Karnal.	
Indian Red Cross Society Distt. Branch, Red Cross Bhavan, Panipat.	Counselling Centre for Drug Addicts Red Cross Bhavan, Panipat.	

Indian Red Cross Society Distt. Branch, Red Cross Bhavan, Rohtak.	Drug De-addiction Centre, Sonipat Road, Rohtak.	

JAMMU & KASHMIR

Society for Promotion of Youth & Massess, Mashwara, 234 Krishna Nagar, Canal Road, Jammu.	Mashwara, 234 Krishna Nagar, Canal Road, Jammu.	

KARNATAKA

CAIM Foundation, 318, 15th Cross, Sada Shiv Nagar, Bangalore.	CAIM Foundation, 318, 15th Cross, Sada Shiv Nagar, Bangalore.	CAIM Treatment and Recovery Centre, Banner - ghatta Road, Hulimavu Village, Bangalore.
Centre for Research in Education, Service and Training for Family, Life Promotion, 14, High Street Bangalore.	CREST Counseling Centre High 14 High Street, Bangalore.	

KERALA

ABHAYA, Vardanandavanam, Trivandrum, Kerala.	ABHAYA, Counselling Centre Poojaappura, Trivandrum.	Bodhi Hospital, De-addiction, Poojaappura, Trivandrum.
International Centre for Study & Development, Shang Village, Valkom, P.O. Quilon.	ICSD Counselling Centre for Drug Addicts, Shangrila Hills, Valikom, Quilon.	
K. Velayudhan Memorial Trust P.B. No. 30, Shertally.	K.V.M. De-addiction and Counselling Centre P.B. No. 30, Shertally.	K.V.M. De-addiction and Counselling Centre, P.B. No. 30, Shertally
Mujahid Educational Trust, 7/852, S.M. Street, P.B. No. 59, Calicut.	Counselling Centre for Drug Addicts, 7/852, S.M. Street, P.B. No. 59, Calicut.	

Organisation	Centre
Total Response to Alcohol and Drug Abuse, Mangam, Kottayam.	TRDADe-addiction-cum-Counselling Centre, Aymanam, P.O. Kottayam.

MADHYA PRADESH

Organisation	Centre
Akhil Bharat Rachnatmak Samaj, E-4/185, Mahavir Nagar near, 10th Bus Stop, Bhopal.	APKE-HI-LIYE, E-4/185, Mahavir Nagar, Behind E-4 Community Hall, near 10th Bus Stop, Bhopal.
Association for Social Health in India, State Branch, Gwalior.	Jagriti Counselling Centre 4, Central Kotwali Road, Ujjain.
Berojgar Mahila Sewa Samiti, Zone-3, Khur Shipar Bhilai, Distt. Durg.	Counselling Centre for Drug Addicts Zone-3, Khurshipar, Bhilai, Distt. Drug.
Gandhi Bhavan, Shyamla Hill, Bhopal.	Navjeevan, De-addiction and Rehabilitation Centre, Gandhi Bhavan, Shyamla Hill, Bhopal.
Indian Red Cross Society Distt. Branch, Prem Kumari Devi Hospital, 9, Biyabani, Indore.	De-addiction Centre, Prem Kumari Devi Hospital, Camp 9, Biyabani, Indore.

MAHARASHTRA

Organisation	Centre
Apanalaya, 75, Bhula Bhai, Desai Road, Bombay	Apnalaya Counselling Centre, Shivaji Nagar, Urban Health Centre, Govandi, Chembur, Bombay

Asha Niketan, 1/7 Urfulla Apartment, Tatekar Lane Opp. Hill Road. Bandra West, Bombay	Counselling Centre for Drug Addicts, Asha Niketan, 1/7, Urfulla Apartment, Tatekar Lane, Opp. Hill Road, Bandra, Bombay	
Drug Abuse Information and Research Centre, H-Block, Sita Ram Building, Ist Floor, Palton Road, Bombay	DAIRRC, H-Block, Sitaram Building, 1st Floor, Palton Road, Bombay	
KRIPA Foundation, Mt. Carmel Church, 81/A, Chapel Road, Bandra, Bombay	Kripa Counselling Centre, Mt. Carmel Church, 81/A, Chapel Road, Bandra, Bombay	Kripa De-addiction Centre, Municipal Hospital, 2nd Floor, Bhadrawadi, Andheri (W), Bombay
Lions Club of Andheri Raj Mahal Building, Andheri-Kurla Road, Andheri (East), Bombay	Lions Club of Andheri, Raj Mahal Building, Andheri-Kurala Road, Andheri (East) Bombay	
Lions Club of Ghatkopar, Lions Community Hall, Garodia (East), Bombay	Hope Centre, C/o YMCA National Society for Clean City, Pant Nagar, Ghatkopar (E), Bombay	
M.S.S. Institute of Social Work, West High Court Road, Bazar Nagar, Nagpur		De-addiction-cum-Rehabilitaion Centre, 49/C Bhagvaghar Layout, Dharmpeth, Nagpur
Muktangan Mitra, Krishna Patrakar Nagar, Pune	Muktangan, Mitra, Counselling Centre Building No. 15, Flat No. 218, Lokmanya Nagar, Pune	

Sevadhan, Municipal Hospital Building, 4th Floor, Bhardwadi, Andheri (W), Bombay	Sevadhan Counselling Centre, Godavari Kripa, Plot No. 169, Ground Floor, Road No. 5, Shivaji Park, Bombay	Sevadhan De-addiction Centre, Municipal Hospital Building, 4th Floor, Bhardawadi, Andheri (W), Bombay
Yuva Shakti Pratishthan, Strihit Vardhani Building, Lokmanya Nagar, Compound, Tilak Bhavan, Kaka Sahab Gadgil Marg, Bombay	Manas Counselling Centre, 1, Manas Clinic Thakar Niwas, 1st Floor, Opp. Pradhan Building, Gokhale Road, near Thane (W), Bombay (near Thane Rly. Station) Manas Counselling Centre-II, Abhinav Sushrut Hospital Ramkuwar Thakar Marg, Near Raja Street, Theatre, Dahisar (E) Bombay	

MANIPUR

Centre for Mental Hygiene, Sangaiprous, Airport Road, Imphal	(i) New Life Changangei, Uchekkon, Airport Road, Imphal (ii) New Life Rangkai, Churachandpur	New Life Changargi Uchekkori, Airport Road, Imphal
Evangelical Convention Church, Lamka	Counselling Centre, Churachandpur	
Manipur Rural Institute, Tera Bazar Sapam Leirak, Imphal	Awakening Home, Tera Bazar, Imphal	
Regional Integrated Rural Development Authority, Sogolband, Loukrakpam, Leikai, Imphal		De-addiction-cum-Rehabilitation Centre, Ukhrul
Service and Education for Welfare Action, Soibam, Leikai, Ayangapalli, Near Jawahar Lal Nehru Hospital, Imphal	'YAIPHAKOL' Soibam, Leikai, Ayangapalli, Near Jawahar Lal Nehru Hospital, Imphal	

MEGHALAYA

Indian Council for Child Welfare, Meghalaya State Branch, 30 Uppar Lachumiere Shillong.	Counselling Centre, 30 Uppar Lachumiere Shillong	

MIZORAM

Faith Home, Chhingchhip, Aizwal	Faith Home (Rinna In) P.O. Chhing Chhip Aizwal	Faith Home (Rinn In), P.O. Chhing Chhip, Aizwal
Mizoram Syond Social Front, Syond Office, Aizwal	Syond Rescue Home cum Counselling Centre, Mission Marg, P.O. Aizwal	
Social Guidance Agency, S.K. Roy's Building, Chandmary West, Aizwal	Social Guidance Agency, Counselling and De-addiction Centre, S.K. Roy's Building, Chandmary West, Aizwal.	Social Guidance Agency, Counselling and Deaddiction Centre, S.K. Roy's Building, Chandmary West, Aizwal

NAGALAND

Bathesda Youth Welfare Centre, Dimapur.	Bathesda Youth Welfare Counselling Centre, P.B. No. 39, Circular Road, Dimapur	Bathesda Youth Welfare Counselling Centre, P.B. No., 39, Circular Road, Dimapur
Nagaland Mother's Association Youth and Women Welfare Organisation, 40, C/o Mrs. L. Hanglu, Kevichusa Residence, Mission Compound, Kohima		
Youth Mission P.B. No. 127, Kohima	Counselling Centre, Tahguist Road, P.B. No. 223, Kohima	

ORISSA

Association of Moral Guide and legal Aid Services for poor, Smriti Saswat Lane At/Po-Nayagrh-752069 Distt. – Puri.	BHARSA Counselling Centre for Drug addicts, At/PO 1/10 Nayagarh, Distt. Puri.	BHARSA, De-addiction cum Rehabilitation Centre At-1/10 Nayagarh, Distt. Puri

Centre for Youth and Social Development, A-70, Saheed Nagar, Bhubaneshwar	Sahara A/154, Ashok Nagar, Bhubaneswar	

PUNJAB

Child Welfare Council, H.No. 15, Sector-3, Chandigarh	Drug Counselling & Rehabilitation Centre, Red Cross Working Women's Hostel, Near Civil Hospital, Batinda	
Indian Red Cross Society, Punjab State Branch, Madhya Marg, Sector- 16/A, Chandigarh	(i) Drug Counselling Centre, Red Cross Bhavan, Distt. Red Cross Branch, Gurdaspur. (ii) Chanan Munra Drug Counselling Centre, Guru Nanak Mission Medical and Educational Trust, Dahan Kaleran, Distt., Jalandhar (iii) Counselling Centre, 958, Phase-III, B-2, Mohali, Ropar	(i) Drug De-addiction Centre (Red Cross), Opp. Thermal Plant Lake, Goniana Road, Bathinda. (ii) Drug De-addiction Centre, 958, Phase-III, B-2, Mohali, Distt. Ropar.
Navjeevani, 61, Model Town, Patiala	Navjeevani Guidance Centre, 192, Punjabi Bagh, Patiala	

RAJASTHAN

Indira Gandhi Mahila Prashikshan Sansthan, Pilani Distt. Jhunjunu	Indira Gandhi Mahila Prashikshan Sansthan, Pilani Distt. Jhunjhunu.	
Manav Kalyan Society, 4/49, Jawahar Nagar, Jaipur	Manav Kalyan Counselling Centre, near Gehlot Nursing Home, Tonk Road, Jaipur	
Opium De-addiction Treatment & Research Trust, P.O. Manaklao Jodhpur	(i) Opium De-addiction and Counselling Centre, Barmer	

	(ii) Opium De-addiction and Counselling Centre, Subhash Nagar, Bhilwara	
	(iii) Opium De-addiction and Counselling Centre, C/o, Shyam Bhavan, near Hotel Haveli Bhiba Pada Jaisalmer	
	(iv) Opium De-addiction and Counselling Centre, near Bus Stand, Jalore	
	(v) Opium De-addiction and Counselling Centre, Rajadadi-ka-nohara, Inside Sojati Gate, Jodhpur	De-addiction Centre P.O. Manakalo Jodhpur

SIKKIM

Association for Social Health in India, State Branch, C/o, State Social Welfare Advisory Board, Kazi Road, Gangtok.	ASHI, Jagriti Counselling and Treatment centre, C/o. State social Welfare, Advisory Board, Kazi Road Gangtok

TAMIL NADU

Association for Social Health in India Tamil Nadu Branch, 30/A, Arcot Street, T. Nagar, Madras	Arogyam, 30/A, Arcot Street, T. Nagar, Madras
CONCERN No. 8, Venkataswamy Street, Panchavati, Chetput, Madras	CONCERN Counselling Centre, 8, Venkataswamy Street Panchavadi P.O. Chetput, Madras

Congregation for the Sisters of the Cross of Chavanod, SOC Sead, P.B. No. 395, Old Goods Shed Road, Teppakulam Tiruchirapalli	SOC Sead Counselling Centre for Drug Addicts P.B. No. 395, Old Goods Shed Road, Tiruchirappalli	
Indian Society of Criminology, Deptt. of Psychology, University of Madras, Madras	(i) Padhu Vazhua No. 11, Lakshman Perumal Mudali Street, Kosapet, Vellore (ii) Padhu Vazhuv 34, MIG, Anna Nagar Cuddalore (iii) Padhu Vazhuv 3/45, Meyyanur Main Road, Five Road, Salem	
Khajamalai Ladies Association Khajamalai, Thruonyrapalli	Khajamalai ladies Association Counselling Centre, Khajamalai Thruonyrapalli	De-addiction Centre, Khajamali
T.T. Ranganathan Clinical Research Foundation, Plot No. 54, Indira Nagar Madras	T.T. Ranganathan Clinical Research Foundation, IV Main Road, Indira Nagar Madras	

TRIPURA

All Tripura Anti-Drug Anti-dowry Social Society Vill. Jangalia P.O. Bislgarh Distt. West Tripura	Tripura Anti-Drug Anti Dowry Social Society, C/o Sri Krishnadhan Roy, Vill. Jangalia, P.O. Bishalgarh, Distt. West Tripura	
Association for social Health in India, Tripura Branch, No. 3, 2nd Lane, Agartala	Jagriti Counselling Centre, Pragati Road Krishnan Nagar Agartala (W) Tripura	

UTTAR PRADESH

Abhinay Repertory Theatre and Research Institute, B-601, Gopala Apartment, 40, Ram Tirath Marg, Lucknow		Inspiration Drug De-addiction Centre B-1, 26 Sector 'A', Aliganj, Lucknow

Association for social Health in India, State Branch, Rani Hotel Bldg., Begam Bridge, Meerut	Jagriti Counselling Centre, Rani Hotel, Begum Bridge, Meerut	
Grama Vikas Sewa Sansthan, 20-B/4A/1 Allapur, Allahabad	Drug Abuse Prevention Counselling Centre, 90E/3 Baghambari Gaddi Allapur, Allahabad.	
Kashi Club, Ganges Bhavan, 14/8, Dasamesh Road, Varanasi	(i) Navchetna Counselling Centre, 1/69, Shastri Nagar, Ghazipur	
	(ii) Navchetna Counselling Centre, Swami Vivekananda Hospital, Bhelupur Crossing Ravindrapuri, Varanasi	Navchetna, Deaddiction Centre, Swami Vivekanand Hospital, Bhelupur Crossing, Varanasi.
	(iii) Navchetna Counselling Centre, Vinayaka Kamacha, Varanasi	Navchetna Drug De-addiction centre, Vinayaka Kamacha, Varanasi
Shri Kanchilal Shastri Smarak Sansthan, C-49, Kalyanpur, Kanpur	Counselling Centre for Drug Addicts C-49, Kalyanpur Kanpur	
Shri Ram Babu Verma Charitable Society, 4/6, Bagh Farzana, Civil Lines, Agra.	Prabhat Counselling Centre, A-14, Kamla Nagar, Agra	Prabhat Deaddiction centre, A-14, Kamla Nagar, Agra

WEST BENGAL

Calcutta Samaritans, 53/3, Elliot Road, Calcutta	Day Care Counselling Centre, Elliot Road, No. 13, Calcutta	

Centre for Psychological and Education Research, 39-C, Sadanand Road, Calcutta		De-addiction-cum-rehabilitation Centre, 39-C, Sadanand Marg, Calcutta
Haldia Samaj Kalyan Parishad, P.O. Anantpur, Via, Suthanta Distt. Midnapore	Drug Counselling Centre, Haldia Samaj Kalyan Road P.O. Durgachak Haldia, Distt. Midnapore	
Human Development and Research Institute, Baurmanpur, 45, Beniatola Calcutta	Counselling Centre, 139/A, Bidhan Saran, Calcutta	
Indian Institute of Human Welfare, BF-240, Salt Lake City, Calcutta	Unmesh, BF-240, Salt Lake City, Calcutta	
Institute of Psychological and Educational Research, 27, Circus Avenue, Calcutta	IPER Drug Centre, 27, Circus Avenue, Calcutta.	
Sir Syed Group of Schools, No. 9, Hossain Shah Road, Calcutta		De-addiction Centre DUVA Drive for United Victory over Addiction, 1, Sourin Roy Rd, Behala, Calcutta
St. Joseph's Rehabilitation and Relief Service, 154, Mahatma Gandhi Rd. Keerapurker, Calcutta	St. Joseph's Rehabilitation & Relief Service, 154, Mahatma Gandhi Road, Keerapuker, Calcutta	
Vivekanand Education Society, 13/3 Kalicharan Dutta Rd. Calcutta.	Vivek Vidhan Counselling Centre, 25/1A, D.H. Road, Behala, Calcutta	Vivek Vidhan Home, 1, Sourin Roy Road, Behala, Calcutta
Women's Co-ordinating Council, 5/1 Red Cross Place, Calcutta	Drug Counselling Centre, 7, Bipinpal Road, Calcutta	

UNION TERRITORIES
CHANDIGARH

Association for Social Health in India, Chandigarh Branch, SCO-6, 1st Floor, Sector 17E, Neelam Cinema Line, Chandigarh	Sujeevan, SCO-6, 1st Floor, Sector 17E, Neelam Cinema Line, Chandigarh	
Young Women's Christian Association of Chandigarh, Sector - 11 B, Chandigarh	YWCA Drug Counselling Centre, Sector-11B, Chandigarh	

DELHI

All-India Association for Social Welfare of Down-trodden, 81, Krishna Gali, Paharganj, Delhi	Counselling Centre 81, Krishna Gali, Paharganj, Delhi	
Association of National Brotherhood for Social Welfare, 21, New Rohtak Road, New Delhi		Jeevan Jyoti Drug De-addiction Centre, RZ-72/5A, Mohan Nagar, Pankha Road, New Delhi
Association for Social Health in India, 4, Deen Dayal Upadhyaya Marg, New Delhi	(i) Jagriti, 4, Deen Dayal Upadhyaya Marg, New Delhi	
	(ii) Jagriti, B-9/65, DDA Flats, Inderlok, Delhi	
	(iii) Jagriti, 15/31-32 Trilok Puri, Delhi	
	(iv) Jagriti, 6562/13, Behind Filmistan, Chamelion Road, Delhi	Ilaj Ghar, H.No. 77831, Chamelion Road, Delhi
	(v) Jagriti, Goenka Road, Near Roshanara Road, Delhi	

	(vi) Jagriti, 2055, Kali Masjid, Turkman Gate, Delhi	
Delhi Women's League, 6, Bhagwan Dass Road, New Delhi	ABHAY-I Counselling Centre, Aruna Nagar (Community Centre), Majnu-Ka-Tilla, Delhi	ABHAY-II, De-addiction and Rehabilitation Centre, C-67/A&B, Bhajan Pura, Near Bus Stop, Delhi
Home Economics Education Society, J-32 South Extension Part-I, Ring Road, New Delhi	(i) Roshni Information Education and Counselling Centre for Prevention of Drug Abuse, C/o Home Economics Education Society, J-32, South Extension, Part-I, Ring Road, New Delhi (ii) Roshni, C/o Sikh Women's Association DDA Building, Tilak Vihar, New Delhi	
Indian Council of Education A-2/59, Safdarjang Enclave, New Delhi	(i) Ankush Counselling Centre, D-1/121, Mochi Bagh, Nanakpura, New Delhi (ii) Jamia Counselling Centre, Jamia Milia Islamia, Jamia Nagar, New Delhi.	i) Ashiana De-addiction Centre, NDMC Poly Clinic, SBS Marg, New Delhi ii) De-addiction Centre Tihar Jail, New Delhi iii) Indian Centre for De-addiction & Rehabilitation, Near Local Shopping Community, Centre, DDA, Slum & J.J. Colony Kalkaji, New Delhi

Society for Promotion of Youth and Masses, P.B. No. 10516, New Delhi	Mashwara, 4021 Pocket-IV, Sector-D, Vasant Kunj, New Delhi	
Dr. Vidya Sagar Kaushalya Devi, Memorial Trust, Nehru Nagar, New Delhi	Dr. Vidyasagar Kaushalya Devi, Memorial Trust Counselling Centre, Drug De-addiction-cum Rehabilitation Centre-D-217, Krishna Park, Khanpur, New Delhi	Dr. Vidyasagar Kaushalaya Devi Memorial Trust, Nehru Nagar, New Delhi
PONDICHERRY		
Association for Social Health in India, H. No. 185, Mahatma Gandhi Road, Pondicherry	Arunodayam, H. No. 185, Mahatama Gandhi Road, Pondicherry	
Indian Women's Council for Social Affaris, No. 30 Trirumalai Road, Lane T. Nagar Madras	ABHAYA OPD Centre, Anglo French Textiles Compound, Cuddalore Road, Pondicherry	

The following are the After-care centres in different States :

GOA : The Shelter, Pooja Mahal, 1st Floor, Ward No. 10, Khorlim, Mapusa, Goa.

MAHARASHTRA : APNALAYA, After-care centre, Wadripada, Dhanjiwali, Rani Sati Marg, Opp. Rateja Complex, Malad (E), Bombay; Day Care Centre, Alandi Road, Yerevada, Pune; Sevadham, C/o Waltas Foundation, Bander of Revdenda Road, Nagaon, Ali Bagh, Ranigarh Distt.

MANIPUR : New Life After-care Centre, Changangai; Uchekkon, Airport Road, Imphal.

NAGALAND : Mount Guild Home, P. Box 160, Kohima.

RAJASTHAN : After-care Centre, P.O. Mahakalo, Jodhpur.

TAMILNADU : T.T. Ranganathan Clinical Research Foundation Afercare Centre, 91, Santhome High Road, Madras.

DELHI : After-care Centre, 67-C, Mohan Nagar, Pankha Road, New Delhi; Day Care Centre, NDMC Poly Clinic, SBS Marg, New Delhi; After-care Centre, DDA Flats, Community Centre, Kalkaji, New Delhi.

Bibliography

Alcoholics Anonymous; Twelve steps and twelve traditions, 1957, N. York. Alcoholics Anonymous World Service.

Allen. D.F.; Jekel J.F.; Crack The Broken Promise 1991, St. Martin's Press, New York.

Allen, D.F., ed. The Cocaine Crisis (1987) pp. 107 ff.

Angst, J.; Personality development and Psychotic complications in drug abuse 1971, Psychosomatic Medicine, 3/2, 3, 146-150.

Ausubel, D.P.; Theory and Problem of Adolescent Adjustment, 1954, Grune and Stratton, N. York.

Balasubrahmanyan, V.; Good girls are bad news, 4th Feb. 1994, The Times of India, N. Delhi.

Balwally, D.; Mizoram now a drug route, Sep. 2, 1993, The Hindustan Times.

Bandura, A. Social Foundations of Thought and Action : A Social Cognitive Theory 1986. Englewood Cliffs, NJ : Prentice Hall.

Bates, W., Dubeck, P. and Larry R., (1969) : "The social context of Urban Narcotic Use." *Proceedings of the Southwestern Sociological Association,* 10, 199-205.

Beaty, J.; Do Humans Need to Get High ? Time, 21 Aug. 1989.

Bennett, L.A., and Ames, G.M.; The American Experience with Alcohol. Contrasting Cultural Perspectives. (Ed.) 1986 Plenum Press, N. Yorks and London.

Black, W.F., and Heald, A., MMPl characteristics of alcohol and illicit drug abusers enrolled in a rehabilitation programme, 1975, Journal of Clinical Psychology, 31, 572-575.

Blumenfield, M. and Glickman, L., (1967) : "Ten Months' Experience with LSD Users Admitted to a County Psychiatric Receiving Hospital," *New York State Journal of Medicine*, 67, 1849-1853.

Blum, R.H. et al; Students and Drugs, 1970, San Francisco, Jossey Bass.

Blum, R., and Richards, L.; Youthful drug use. In : Dupont R.I. : Goldstein, A.; and O'Donnell, J., Eds. Handbook on Drug Abuse, National Institute on Drug Abuse, Washington D.C. 1979, Supt. of Does, U.S. Govt. Print Off. p. 257-267.

Brehem, M.L. and Back, K.W. Self Image and attitudes towards drugs – 1968. Journal of Personality., 36 : 299-314.

Carmichael, J.S., Linn, N.W., Pratt, T. and Webb, N.; Self-concept and substance abuse treatment, 1977, Comprehensive Psychiatry, 18/4, 357-362.

Cockett, R., and Marks, V.; Amphetamines taking among young offenders, 1969, British Journal of Psychiatry, 115, 1203-1204.

Coleman, J.C.; Abnormal Psychology and Modern Life, 1976, Scott, Foresman and Company USA.

Crooks and Stein : Psychology; Science, Behaviour and Life, 1988, Holt, Rinehart and Winston, INC. New York.

Curran, D. and Patridge, M.; Psychological Medicine; An Introduction to Psychiatry 1959, E. and S. Livingston Ltd. Edinburgh.

Dorus, W., and Senay, E.; Depression, demographic depression, and drug abuse, 1980, American Journal of Psychiatry, 137, 24-36.

Drug Abuse Prevention, Directory of voluntary organisations funded by Govt. of India, Ministry of Welfare, 1991, DAVP, N. Delhi.

Dusek, D. and Gindano, D.; Drugs : A Factual Account, 1980. Reading, MA : Addison-Wesley.

Emblad, H.; WHO study on substance abuse, report in use of drug rising among street children 14th March 1994, Hindustan Times.

Falco, M.; The making of a Drug Free America, programmes that work, 1992. Times Books Inc. New York.

Falewicz. J. K., (1970) : "Social Determinants of Alcohol Consumption among the Polish Youth," *Sociological Abstracts*, 789.

Fernandez, C.; Drug trafficker married women to use them as carriers, 16th Aug. 1994, The Times of India, N. Delhi.

Gawin, F.M. and Kleber, H.D.; Abstinence Symptomatology and Psychiatric diagnosis in chronic cocaine users, 1986, Archives of General Psychiatry, 43, 107-13.

Gerald, D.L., and Kornotsky, C.; A social psychiatric study of adolescent opiate addicts, 1954, Psychiatric Quarterly. 28, 113- 125.

Gergen, K.; The concept of self, 1971, New York.

Ghosh, S.K.; Behind Delhi's narcotics boom. Jan. 24, 1994, The Hindustan Times.

Gilbert, J.G. and Lombardi, D.N., (1967) : "Personality Characteristics of Young Male Narcotic Addicts," *Journal of Consulting Psychology*, 31, 536-38.

Goodwin, D.W., Schulsinger, F., Hermansen, L., Guze, S.B., Winokur, G.; Alcohol problems in adoptees raised apart from alcoholic biological parents. Arch-Gen. Psychiat., Feb. 1973, 28(2), 238-43.

Goodwin, D.W.; Schulsinger, F., Moller, N., Hermansen, L., Winokur, G.; Guze, S.B. Drinking problems in adopted and non- adopted sons of alcoholics Aug. 1974. Arch. Gen. Psychiat., 31(2), 164-69.

Gossop, M.; Drug dependence and self-esteem, 1976, International Journal of Addiction, 11/5, 741-753.

Gross, W.F., and Alder, L.O.; Aspects of alcoholic's self- concepts as measured by the Tennesse self-concept scale, 1970, Psychological Report, 27, 431-434.

Hall, S.M., Wasserman, D.A., Havassy, B.E.; Relapse Prevention, NIDA Research Monograph series-Improving Drug Abuse Treatment- 106, 1991.

Hartgen, C.A., and Hill, H.E.; Effects of morpheric and phenobarbitual on differential MMPl profiles, 1959, Journal of Clinical Psychology, 15, 434-437.

Hogan, R. Mankin, D., Conway, J., and Fox, S.; Personality correlates of undergraduate marijuana use, 1970, Journal of Counselling and Clinical Psychology, 35, 58-63.

Hurlock, E.B.; Child Development, 1975, McGraw-Hill, Kogakusha Ltd.

Hurlock, E.B., (1956) : *Child Development*, New York : Mcgraw-Hill. (1974) : *Developmental Psychology*, New Delhi : Tata-Mcgraw-Hill.

Jekél, J.F.; Public health approaches to the cocaine problem, in D.F. Allen ed. The Cocaine Crisis, 1987, 107 ff.

Jeroma, F., Carrol, X.C., Klein, I.M., and Santo, Y.; Comparison of the similarities and differences in the self-concepts of male alcoholics and addicts, 1978. Journal of Consulting and Clinical Psychology, 46/3, 575-576.

Kandel, D.B.; Convergencies in prospective longitudinal surveys of drug use in normal populations, in Longitudinal Research on Drug use : Empirical Findings and Methodological Issues, 1978, N. York, Hemisphere.

Kandel, D.B., Treiman, D., Faust, R., Single, E.; Adolescent Involvement in Legal and Illegal Drug use, a Multiple Classification Analysis, Social Forces 55 : 438-58, 1956.

Kaplan, H.B.; Antecedents of Deviant Responses : Predicting from a General Theory of Deviant Behaviour, Journal of Youth and Adolescence 6 : 89-101 (1977).

Kapur, T.; Drug Epidemic among Indian Youth – A study of drug addicts, 1985., Concept, N. Delhi.

Kataria, R.P.; The Narcotic Drugs and Psychotropic substances Act, 1985, Orient Law House.

Kennedy, T.D.; Kimura, H.K.; Transfer, behavioral improvement and anxiety reduction in systematic desensitization. Oct. 1974. J. Cons. Clin. Psychol. 42(5), 720-28.

Khan, M.Z.; Drug Use Amongst The College Youth, 1985, Somiya Pub.

Kielhotz, P., and Ladewig, D.; Drug dependence of young people, 1970, cited in Psychiatry Digest, Sept. 1970, 31, 29.

Kirpekar, S.; Drug menace spreading its tentacles, 5th March, 1994, The Times of India.

Knight, R.G., and Prout, C.T.; A study of results in hospital treatment of drug addiction, 1955, in Edward Podolsky (Ed.), Management of Addictions, Philosophical Library, New York.

Lewis, A.R. and Albert, J.R. Jr., (1969) : "Apathy, Truancy and Delinquency as Adaptations to School Failure," *Social Forces*, 48, 12-22.

Lewis, B., (1973); *The Sexual Powers on Marijuana*, New York : Wyden.

Linton, H. and Graham, E.; Personality correlates of persuasibility 1959, pp. 69-101, in C. Hovland and I. Janis (eds). Personality and Persuasibility, New Haven; Yale University Press.

Long, R.E.; Drugs and American Society (Ed.) 1986, The H W. Wilson Company, New York.

Manning, M.; The Drugs Menace, 1985, Columbus Books Great Britain.

Mausner, J., Kramer, S.; Epidemiology : An Introductory Text, 2nd Edn. (Philadelphia : W.B. Saunders, 1985.

McClelland, D.C., Dawis, W.N., Kalin, R., and Wanner, E.; The drinking man, 1972, New York, The Free Press.

McDill, T.H., (1965) : "Interpersonal Relationships and the Alcoholic," *Proceedings of the Fourth South-Eastern School of Alcohol,* 97-107.

Meador, B., and Rogers, C. (1984) Person-centred therapy. In R. Corsini (Ed.) Current Psychotherapies. Itasca, IL : Peocock.

Mitra, A.; Drug scene on campus gets murkier Feb. 21, 1994, The Hindustan Times.

Mohan, D., Sethi, H.S., Tongue, E., Current Research in Drug Abuse in India (series II), 1985, I.K. Printer, Delhi.

Mondal, J.; Women, their families and drugs, 1992, in Rise in drug addiction among city women, 18 Sep. 1992, Statesman.

Nair, J.; where opium taking is status symbol, Dec. 4, 1993, The Hindustan Times.

National Crime Prevention Council, Challenges and Opportunities in Drug Prevention, A demand reduction resource guide for law enforcement officers, U.S. deptt. of Justice, 1990. U.S.A.

NIDA Capsules; Resources to address drugs in the workplace, Aug. 1990, U.S. Deptt. of Health and Human Services.

— The Drug-free workplace Act of 1988; July 1991.

Nyswander, M. The Drug Addict as a Patient, New York City Department of Health, 1956, Grunne and Stratton : New York and London.

Padmam, M.S.R.; An investigation into the effect of illicit drug use on certain personality factors, 1986, thesis, Kerala Univ. Trivandrum.

Parades, A., Ludwig, K.D., Hassanfeld, I.N. and Cornelison, F.S.; A clinical study of alcoholics using audio-visual image feedback, 1969, Journal of Nervous and Mental Disease, 148/4, 449-456.

Paton, S., Kessler, R., Kandel, D., Depressive Mood and Adolescent Illicit Drug Abuse : A Longitudinal Analysis, Journal of Genetic Psychology 131 : 267-89 (1977)

Paton, S.M., and Kandel, D.B., Psychological factors and adolescent illicit drug use : Ethinicity and sex differences, 1978, Adolescence, 13/50, 187-200.

Perls F.; The Gestalt Approach, 1973. Palo Alto, CA : Science and Behaviour Books.

Perls, F.; Theory and Technique of Personality Integration, 1948. American Journal of Psychotherapy, 2, 656-686.

Pickens, R.W., Leukefeld, C.G., Schuster, C.R.; NIDA Research Monograph 106, 1991.

Prashant, S.; Drug Abuse and Society; 1993, Ashish Publishing House, N. Delhi.

Pratt, B.; Studies reveal alcoholism differs in males and females, July 1972, APA Monitor, 3(7), 1.

Rado, S, (1933) : "The Psychoanalysis of Pharmocothymia (Drug Addiction)," *Psychiatric Quarterly,* 2, 1-23.

Rauch fleisch, U.; Psychodynamic aspects of alcohol and drug addiction, 1971, cited in Psychiatry Digest, 32, 20.

Razeena Padman, M.S.; An investigation into the effect of illicit drug use on certain personality factors, 1985.

Report on Aids carrier eunuchs are potent, 14th March, 1994, The Times of India.

Report on Arts Control in curbing drug menace urged, Jan. 9, Hindustan Times.

Report of the International Narcotics Control Board for 1993, United Nations Publications.

Report on Heroin abuse spreading in India, 5 March, 1994, Hindustan Times.

Report on – Trafficking of drugs on the rise in N-E., 5 Jan., 1994, Hindustan Times.

Robbins, P.R.; Depression and drug addiction, 1974, Psychiatry Quarterly, 48, 374-386.

Robins, L.; Helzer, J., Weissman, M.; Orvaschel, H.; Guenberg, E; Burke, J.; Regier, D.; Lifetime prevalence of specific psychiatric disorders in three sites, 1984. Archives of General Psychiatry, 41, 949-958.

Rogers, C. Client centered therapy. In I. Kutash and A. Wolf (Eds). Psychotherapist's Casebook. San Francisco : Josey-Bass.

Rosenberg, M.; Society and the Adolescent Self-Image. 1965. Princeton, N.J. Princeton University Press.

Roslyn, G. and George, S., (1968) : "Complementary Pathology in Families of Male Heroin Addicts," *Social Casework,* 49, 356-361.

Rounsaville, B. Weissman, M., Wilber, C. et. al., The heterogeneity of psychiatric diagnosis in treated opiate addicts, 1982, Arch. Gen. Psychiatry, 39, 161-166.

Sain, B.; Drug Danger and Social Behaviour – New challenges, 1988, Sharda Prakashan Delhi.

Sanjivi, K.S.; Only one life, 1974, Bhartiya Vidya Bhawan, Bombay.

Saunders, B., and Allsop, A.; Relapse : A Psychological Perspective Br. J. Addict 82 : 417-429, 1987.

Shanmugam, T.E.; Personality factors underlying drug abuse among college students, 1979, Psychological studies, 24/1, 24-34.

Sinha, S. and Suri, A.; The drug-connection-series;

— A cross-border web that defies all dragnets, 1994, Indian Express N. Delhi.

— The police-mafia nexus smoothens all hindrances, 1994, Indian Express, N. Delhi.

Smart, R.G. and Jones, D.; Foundation, Toronto, Ontario, Illicit L.S.D. Users, their personality characteristics and psychopathology, 1970, Journal of Abnormal Psychology, 75, 286- 292.

Smart, R.G.; The relationship between intellectual deterioration, extraversion and neuroticism among chronic alcoholics, 1965, Journal of Clinical Psychology, 21, 27-29.

Soares, A., Soares, L.; Self-description and adjustment correlates of occupational choice, 1965, Journal or Educational Research 6 : 27-31.

Srinivasa, S.; Smoke to be free, June 19, 1994, The Sunday Times of India Review.

Subramaniam, S.; Drug addiction among the student community in the city of Madras, 1980, Madras School of social work.

Suresh, N.; one third of cancer patients linked to tobacco use, 8 Sep., 1994, Times of India.

The third triennial report on Drug Abuse and Drug Abuse Research, 1991, DHHS Publications, USA.

UNDP in India, Report, 1993.

UNI Backgrounder, Drug Abuse, April 21, 1988 Vol. XIII, No. 16.

UNI Backgrounder, Narcotics Traffic in India, April 14, 1988, Vol. XIII, No. 15.

Way, L. W., (1970) : *The Drug Scene : Help or Hang-up* ? Englewood Cliffs : Prentice-Hall.

Wechsler, H.; Alcohol intoxication and drug use among teenagers, 1976, J. Stud. Alcohol, 37 (11), 1672-1677.

Wiener, R.S.P., (1970) : *Drugs and School Children,* London : Longman.

Wilker, A.; Opiate Addiction; Psychological and neuro- physiological aspects in relation to clinical problems, 1963 springfield, I 11 : CC Thomas.

Williams., A.F. : Self concept of college problem drinkers : A comparison with alcoholics-1965-Quarterly Journal of Studio on Alcohol, 26/4 : 586-594.

Wilsnack, S.C.; Feminity by the bottle, 1973, Psych. Today, Apr. 6 (11), 39-43; 96 (a).

Wilsnack, S.C.; Sex role identity in female alcoholism, 1973, J. Abnorm. Psychol; Oct. 82 (2), 253-61, (b).

Wilson, G.; Your Personality and Potential – the illustrated guide to self-discovery, 1989, Salem House Publishers, Topsfield, Massachusetts.

Wilson, R.A.; (1973) : *Sex and Drugs,* Mayflower.

Wilson, S., and Kennard, D.; The extraverting effect of treatment in a therapeutic community for drug abusers, 1978, The British Journal of Psychiatry, 132, 296-299.

Winokur, G.; Reich, T.; Rimmer, J., Pitts, F.N.; Jr. Alcoholism. III : diagnosis and familial psychiatric illness in 259 alcoholic probands, 1970. Arch. Gen. Psychiat : 23 (2), 104-11.

Woody, G.E., and Blaini, J.; Depression in narcotics addicts; Quite possible more than a chance association. In : Dupont R.; Goldstein, A : and O'Donnell, J., eds. Handbook on Drug Abuse, National Institute on Drug Abuse. Washington, D.C., Supt. of Docs, U.S. Govt. Print, Off., 1979.

Yost, O.R., (1954) : *The Bane of Drug Addiction,* New York : Macmillan.

Ziegler, J., Scientists ponder drinkers, drinks, differences. 1984. The Oregonian, July 5.

Zuckerman M., Neary, R.S., Brustman, B.A.; Sensation seeking Scale Correlates in Experiences (Smoking, Drugs, Alcohol, Hallucinations and Sex) and Preference for complexity (Design) in Proceedings of the 78th Annual Convention of the American Psychological Association, Vol. 5 1970.